CW01099689

The Art of Tennis ^{II}

An Exploration of Planet Tennis

Dominic J. Stevenson

An imprint of Bennion Kearny Ltd.

Dedicated to Jacky and John

Table of Contents

The Swan Show

What went before is gone. What matters is the here and now, the present showdown, the infinity of a moment, of this one. Switch on, don't miss a thing, there is only this.

A black screen. The gentle sound of soft water being moved through. Minimal. Almost nothing.

Enter the swans, all peace and ripples as the bodies – one in the foreground and another fading, shrinking behind – drift across the water. The water turns from darkness to a familiar plush green, and the Wimbledon tale begins to change.

As though it were an arrow into one's consciousness, a violin enters the fray, echoing the swans' movement, graceful as they go, perfecting the piece. The four-stringed fiddle is joined by other sweeping instruments.

The swans then burst into human forms – our most recognised tennis players – as they explode into all manner of shots, accompanied by orchestral overtones. The music then switches to an explosive techno beat, met by the players striving for greatness. Every sinew and every muscle is trained to contract and react accordingly. This is the pièce de résistance of art, of pulchritude, of nature at its richest. A well of endless, sourced magic.

The players revert to the swans and the dramatic ballet continues. Changes appear, in pose of creature and shot, flicking the switch between the classical piece and the techno burst each time the visuals change. Flurries inspire the senses; they awaken the memories and undiluted nostalgia.

The wind kicks up, rustles the leaves in the full-bodied trees – or is it applause – lifting the players. The swans take off, winged creatures on their flight paths.

Finish on a piano, accompanied by the end credits screen, with the name of the tournament and its year. Coming soon – an advert of drama, of passion, of echoing beauty, filling the audience, now awaiting the arrival of another major; another beautiful fortnight, with bated breath.

As the final piano note falls, as it hits the ground like the last raindrop, and the next advert or program begins, Wimbledon has reached inside the chest, stirred the very passions it is famous for and warmed the heart. All at once, once again. A brief snapshot of The Swan Show is over. The Swan Show will commence again shortly...

A Brief Analysis of Rafael Nadal's Grass Court Prospects

From outside the Nadal bubble, it appeared that, when he was younger, it didn't enter his head that he couldn't win on any surface; it was a question of improving his game and achieving his goal. Now, and based on his Wimbledon exits since his last title at the All England Club in 2010 (and appearance in the final again the following year), it seems that the thought process is deeper, and his ability to talk himself out of his chances has an impact. He has repeatedly lost to far inferior players. Wimbledon has long since started to feel like a rut that only he can break.

The clay court season has indubitably worn him out somewhat, but there's no question that he turns up at Wimbledon every year because it has value to him, and he wants to leave his mark there again. It's not purely nostalgia. He understands the importance of the only major played on grass, and given his eventual first title there in 2008 – by way of an epic five-setter with Federer – it holds a special place in his heart. That final was, of course, one of the finest tennis matches ever played in the tournament.

How realistic is it to expect or hope for Nadal to go deep into the draw? Well, each year brings up the same question and then qualifies it as a futile expectation for him to win the title as he is defeated in, or before, the round of sixteen.

Those in Nadal's camp, his loyal fan base, remain expectant and positive. They want to see Federer's renewed reign at Wimbledon questioned and even toppled by Nadal finding his grass court form from the decade before. It's been almost 10 years now since he was good on grass, and his body, his career, and his confidence have all entered different phases to the one he was in throughout his early to late twenties. He is now 32 years of age, with ongoing injury niggles and larger concerns. The grass court season becomes more and more of a challenge and disruption, perhaps, to his annual targets. That also brings into question whether the grass court season deserves more time and a bigger tournament or two – such as a Masters played on grass – to let the players properly bed themselves in on the surface, before they then move on and back to the hard courts that the first three or so months of the season are played on.

Some of his game, here on grass, wherever, leaves the audience almost speechless. He has a range of shots in his arsenal befitting his status as a modern sporting matador or gladiator. All the praise heaped on his shoulders is deserved. Wouldn't it be great to see a grass court swansong before he heads off into the distance?

THE
WIMBLEDON
AISLE

Action on the Outer Courts

Due to the vastness of the Grand Slams, the first week can be a thoroughly good moment to get down to the venue – such as Wimbledon this week – and catch some splendid scenes on the outer courts. The second week of men's and women's singles is predominantly played on the chief courts with the larger capacities, but finding some well-known names in more unexpected places during the first week can feel like a successful treasure hunt, especially for unsuspecting fans. In fact, the first day has the potential to be a genuine treat. The plush green grass of London's world-famous All England Club sees many of the top names not only playing, but coming from, and going to, the practice courts. Preparation turns into tournament action, as things become exciting. Players, put your game faces on, grab your racket bags and hit that ball like you mean it; like you understand the singular mission, because you never know if it's the last chance.

It isn't only Centre Court and Court One that have seen classic matches over the years. You never quite know when something will turn out to be an incredibly memorable encounter between two of the world's finest, or even include a brave wild card or qualifier (who has already come through three matches the previous week). The uncertain outcomes of the outer court contests are what makes them every inch the equal of those more royally selected pairings that take place on the better-known courts.

Explore! There is much to see and many players to discover. The Grand Slams have the most players in the main singles' draws, bringing an opportunity to find obscure names and faces that might just break through in future years, or even right before your very eyes this year at Wimbledon. Who imagined Marco Cecchinato would have that run at the recent Roland Garros? Finding him on a lesser-known court, in the earlier rounds, might just warm the hearts of fans later in the event. Treasure is found in the strangest of places. Especially in Grand Slam tennis. It isn't all safe predictions and certainty. In sport, anything can happen on the day.

An Early Centre Court Four-Set Thriller

Everybody knew, on paper, that a first-round meeting on day one of the 2018 Wimbledon Championships between three-time Grand Slam champion, Stanislas Wawrinka, and the current holder of the ATP Finals title, Grigor Dimitrov, had the potential to be a thriller. Switzerland's Wawrinka might have had a poor year or so, since reaching the Roland Garros final of 2017, but when he finds his groove – on the big occasion – he often has a way of cranking up the speed and accelerating into terrain that makes him hard to catch, almost impossible to compete with.

Therefore, the much lower-ranked Swiss maestro emerged, arms aloft, for a victory – 1-6, 7-6, 7-6, 6-4 – that didn't seem likely at the close of the first set. Especially when you factor in that he had been dispatched with ease, only last week, by the returning Andy Murray at the Eastbourne International. Despite Wawrinka's past glories, nobody was expecting too much from him. To beat Dimitrov, who has a past-proven grass court pedigree, was one of the shocks of the day. Wimbledon, the only major still eluding the Swiss, is surely out of sight? It's his least favourite surface and he is now well into his thirties, just hoping to get back to competing with the very top players regularly again. As for the other majors, well, time will tell what he is still able to achieve.

The Tired Tennis Player

An early exit. Too many warm-up tournaments. A good run at one. Potential revealed to all, if they hadn't already tuned in to it. Perhaps they already had an inkling? But your legs felt heavy and your hitting was sluggish. Aryna Sabalenka looked like a face for the future of Wimbledon – and, of course, she still is, having only just turned 20 last week. She was runner up to Caroline Wozniacki in the Nature Valley event in Eastbourne. Seagulls squawking and cawing overhead provided a fitting backdrop as she took flight on grass, hinting at what might yet lay in wait. Today, however, she has fallen at the first hurdle on only day one of the Championships, to the sterling challenge of the increasingly difficult to beat Romanian 29th seed Mihaela Buzarnescu. After seeing out a tight first set, on a tie-break, Sabalenka then proceeded to lose the second set badly. Tellingly, she let her grip of set three go in the final stages, just when she had started to claw her way back from a gulf in games. She couldn't quite pull it off.

You've played a lot of matches recently, you've brought yourself into form, hitting your way there, but simultaneously you have worn yourself out. Sadly, this becomes manifest at the main event –the one circus everyone wants to be the ringleader of.

You tune in and out of form all year round, a never-ending tempest of challenges. Whilst the bodies grow stronger, the mind also needs to progress. Modern tennis for the young is an increasingly steep hill to climb to reach the summit. Much is known that can take a player to the top, in addition to ability and hard work, but there are junctures at which the physicality and constant high-level pressure take their toll. That's only natural.

All White

You know where you are. Everyone does. The dress code does that; it sends you back in time with fond reminiscences of previous visits, of matches marked upon the memory, even of a magical summer.

The all white uniform of the players participating at the All England Lawn Tennis and Croquet Club Championships represents a dignity and traditions held firm, ones that date back, an identity for the ages. Wimbledon is not like others, Wimbledon does not want to follow. It quite simply leads the way.

The most unique of all tennis events.

There is an air of predictability, of the strict uniform, as players almost dress the same. There's little room for creativity but an old-fashioned elegance is present that is not seen elsewhere. In an ever-changing world some things simply have no need to. Here, the tennis speaks volumes and nothing else matters.

The Opening Action of Day Three

Well, fireworks have already been seen, in just two immaculately sunshine-laden days at the All England Club during the start of the 2018 Championships. All the round one matches of both the men's and women's singles draws have been completed. That is 128 matches in total, half belonging to each gender. 64 players on each side have already gone out, and 64 have gone through, but unlike every other year the weather has made it feel like being elsewhere. There's not a wisp of a cloud in sight, and England has simultaneously pushed its way – somehow – into the quarter-finals of the men's football World Cup over in Russia.

Magic is in the air.

It isn't about what is to come but celebrating the here and now. That isn't to say that magnificence doesn't await. Who knows? We only truly have the present moment. And there has been treasure aplenty to discover across the courts at SW19 already this year, from Serena Williams' return and Roger Federer unveiling his brand new sponsor Uniqlo, to Daniil Medvedev surprising the 16th seeded Borna Ćorić in straight sets, and Donna Vekić beating Sloane Stephens in two.

And, now, here begins the second round of this year's chief grass court tournament. The baselines are being battered by a seldom-seen London sun, as well as the usual dancing footsteps of the players making their way through the draw. Most forget to venture in to the net, to mix it up, to challenge the opponent with that aspect of the game.

The Centre Court Azarenka and Plíšková Contest

One is still returning to her best after childbirth, and a lengthy delay due to off-court drama holding back the next phase of her playing career. One has not proven herself, thus far, to have grass court pedigree, despite being well and truly lodged in the upper echelons of the WTA rankings. She even grazed the number one ranking last year. It did not last. But it spoke of the player's wider ability and potential, still yet to be entirely fulfilled.

This match would see one of the two players – hence its status as the opening match on Centre Court on the first Wednesday of this year's event – push into round three. That would be a big and rewarding step for either lady.

Victoria Azarenka, a double Grand Slam champion, versus Karolína Plíšková, a superb server, whose game is potentially well-suited to the green grass of the All England Club. If she could make her game a little more solid and consistent, she would fashion herself as one of the chief women to beat at the 2018 edition of the year's third major.

Plíšková wins, finally getting past round two on the grass of Wimbledon – having lost in the second round the previous five years; Azarenka succumbs to a painful defeat that indicates she has a way still to go. Plíšková is more match fit, more into the groove of the tour, and no doubt determined to put the ghost of her past failures here to rest. A short but sweet post-match off-court interview with Plíšková reveals her thoughtful and inspired side as she calmly enjoys ending her second-round hoodoo. And then she is gone, into round three for the first time.

What a Turnaround!

Guido Pella has thus far – at two sets apiece – managed to turn his second-round match against last year's runner-up Marin Čilić on its head. It's a different day now – the airwaves are different, it's another frequency, a strange vibe growing, and anything can happen. The rain interrupted play yesterday evening and, in the new day, Argentine Pella has continued to force the issue and push Čilić from his comfort zone.

Previously, Swiss star Stanislas Wawrinka lost in straight sets to Thomas Fabbiano shortly before, and such a comeback as Pella's own – which in Wawrinka's match had briefly seemed more likely – failed to materialise.

Five-set thrillers are common in the men's second round here today. Several of yesterday's matches clung on for dear life through the rain delay and seemed to be altered by that pause. Matches carried over from Wednesday evening are seeing brilliant endings, and Pella v Čilić was the one to end them all.

Pella had been two sets to love down yesterday, in the early evening, when the rains came. He had managed to hang on and a rain delay came to his aid, with all to play for today. But other than his own camp, not many could have really expected what unfolded, what became reality. For Pella did indeed go on to despatch last year's finalist, Marin Čilić, swinging like his life depended upon it, giving it his all, absolutely deserving of his biggest career win to date. As he himself would state, the reason for the win was his aggression and fight for every ball. That's the beauty of Grand Slam tennis and just goes to show how consistency in the majors is almost unfathomably difficult. It's difficult to comprehend, to analyse, and to achieve.

Another seed has been buried, a shock, but a memory already. With the unpredictable at many a turn, Wimbledon keeps us all on our toes.

Tsitsipas Has Got Game!

Stefanos Tsitsipas has got grass court game. Hot on the heels of a brilliant clay court season in which he genuinely announced himself, he has today reached the second week – and the fourth round – of Wimbledon. He reminds me of the past, and he also indicates the future and how bright it is. Strictly speaking, though, there is no 'future of tennis'. There is what has gone before, and there is the present. Many have succumbed to being labelled the future of the sport and failed to deliver for one reason or another; players such as Grigor Dimitrov, Anna Kournikova, and Bernard Tomic. It isn't easy to realise potential and withstand the multitude of challenges and problems that a tennis career can provide.

What with the Becker-esque on-court diving, and the Borg hairband, and draping locks, you could be forgiven for thinking he is an amalgamation of greatest hits from the past rolled into a tall, slim Greek god of tennis. Someone who floats around the court with a heart-on-his-sleeve desire, oozing talent and charm.

Age is always a hot topic of conversation for those working in tennis and assessing future hopes, but much is determined by temperament on the big stage. Some don't have that at any age, some are born with it. Tsitsipas looks like one of those players who is completely natural and at home in the big match setting; his game even excelling there. His reactions to the crowd, pumping them up when the mood demands it, mark him as one to watch now. Forget about tomorrow, he is exactly what the tour needs today. Precisely the kind of character to move the game past the legends at the top, who can surely not last too much longer (can they?).

The Silence Before Another Storm

Wimbledon pauses, Middle Sunday is silent, the bodies of the public absent, all is calm before the storm. This is the quiet that provides a louder thump and pop to proceedings in the following days – that enables a monumental Monday in which all remaining singles players, in both the men's and women's singles play, and the draws look to clearly establish who is in and who is out. Who will be the faces of the final days of the event?

The Brilliantly Overloaded Order of Play / The TV Schedule

Manic, or Magic, Monday is spilling over with action across the tennis courts of Wimbledon. To even reach the second week is an achievement, but of course, you want to take that momentum into a charge towards the title. The lack of remaining top female seeds is unusual to say the least.

Karolína Plíšková's earlier fourth-round exit has ensured that the quarter-finals will – for the first time – include not one of the tournament's top ten seeded players. Angelique Kerber is the highest remaining seed, at 11, and Serena Williams (25th seed) is the most successful past champion – now the favourite, surely.

The order of play is chock-full of the top singles matches, as today is the sole day on which every remaining player in both the gentlemen's and ladies' draws is seen in action. At one stage, six matches are in progress at once. It means that much great action is missed, as we don't have enough eyes, simultaneous channel possibilities, or bodies to attend all the relevant courts.

Wimbledon and the BBC – the love affair, thankfully, continues. However, what was screened – looking back on past days – all too often, was limited to the chief courts of Centre and Number One. On a day like today, with so much singles action across six of the courts – and so many talented players that UK tennis fans rarely see – the red button enables all-court access to pick the matches, abilities, and antics you want to watch.

The TV schedule of yore was far too safe and not at all progressive. The modern saturation of media and technological access means much more of Wimbledon is available in many new ways. Wimbledon is a traditional event, but some of the players, essentially hidden from the bigger crowds on the main two courts and, once upon a time, the television audience, also deserve the limelight as they carve their way through the draw. Federer matches are mostly processional, and an encounter of something like Isner (recent Masters winner) v Tsitsipas (19-year-old Greek dynamo), for example, on occasion, would open the eyes of existing and new fans alike. The lead channels still show those main court meetings rather than an array of what is on offer, but at least we can pick and choose now. We get to decide rather than having it decided for us.

The Fall of King Roger

Unfortunately, I spent a substantial portion of one of the finest men's quarter-finals' days in the skies, travelling. I was in-between A and B, in sporting spectator limbo, missing the Court One and Centre Court action, as classic encounters were played.

Once my plane had landed, the BBC live feed was updated and the news that Roger Federer and Kevin Anderson were level at 5-5 in the final set stunned me. When I last looked, Federer had been 4-2 up in the second set tie-break, only three points from claiming the second set for a two-sets-to-love lead over the giant South African. For me it felt as good as over, done and dusted, as so many other matches in which Federer had taken a 2-0 set lead, had also ended so comprehensively and predictably. How it had turned on its head, well, obviously in great part down to Anderson's character and never-say-die attitude, seemed unfathomable.

Federer's thus far serene progress had made the entire men's tournament seem stale, but the Swiss master's fans happy. His half of the draw seemed straightforward and no name – despite the undeniable ability of Anderson and John Isner (the last two remaining players on that half of the draw) – stood out as a potential victor over Roger in such imperious form. Did he underestimate his opponents? Did he get too big for his already sizeable boots? Did he succumb to the five-set format, having been untested over a lengthier period in his previous four matches? Did he lose his way, as his game was pulverised into submission by Anderson? How much was Federer, and how much was Anderson? Did it even matter with such a shock result? So many questions!

2-6, 6-7, 7-5, 6-4, 13-11 it ended.

On the women's side, all top ten seeds had fallen by the end of the second Monday of play, and yet Federer v Anderson was *the* shock of the Championships. It had often felt like the draw, the court schedule, and many other factors were designed to aid the grand old king of Wimbledon to move into the final and claim another title. Therefore, this was greatly refreshing and eye-catching for the neutral to witness.

John Isner had earlier beaten Milos Raonic and would find himself up against Anderson, and not Federer, in the semi-final to come. Nadal beat Del Potro in a 5-set epic. Over 4 hours.

Nadal a set up.

Nadal 2-1 down.

Nadal conquers in a tight classic.

Djokovic beat Nishikori in 4. Djokovic looking back to his best, or almost there.

What a day!

Women's Semi-Finals

The women's semi-final matches were unbalanced and something of an anti-climax. Just like the England World Cup football match from the night before, that was still echoing its doom and gloom into today. As Angelique Kerber and Serena Williams took their places in the final – a re-match of the final two years ago – by out-muscling and diminishing the abilities of Jelena Ostapenko and Julia Görges respectively, what had been a rather peculiar ladies' tournament suddenly made perfect sense. Everything was in place.

The two matches took only the fewest sets possible, each just over an hour in duration, and neither sucking the crowd into the encounter with the pendulum of drama awake and swinging between the two players. There was none of that.

The two semi-finals were heavily outweighed, the experience of the two older ladies was telling, and that difference has brought two women – who in 2016 seemed to need each other's competitiveness – back into each other's sight. Only 24 months previously, each player was the biggest challenge either could face. And not only did Kerber's poor 2017 reflect someone uncomfortable at the top of the game, but also, I had a feeling she greatly missed the ultimate test of Serena's game.

Battle of the Big Serves /
Battle of the Greats

Even on paper, you couldn't have two more contrasting semi-finals, style-wise, than those in the men's singles at Wimbledon this second Friday of the Championships. The big serve-fest of John Isner against Kevin Anderson, followed by the mental and physical battle between undeniably two of the greats of the game – of modern tennis, of all tennis – Rafael Nadal and Novak Djokovic.

However, despite predictions of tie-break after tie-break in a boring Isner v Anderson match, unravelling slowly as an hors d'oeuvre, it is as much the main course as the following match will be. This first semi-final alone is well on target to take twice as long as both ladies' semi-finals of the day before, put together.

Isner and Anderson have just entered a final set. Someone will get out of it alive, someone with their Wimbledon dream in tatters. Someone will await Nadal or Djokovic in Sunday's final. Someone will be tired, in need of a rest, after playing so many sets in the past few days. Someone will be in unknown territory in their early thirties. The big serves are there, but there is also much greater entertainment and drama than people, generally, had perhaps predicted, as they become embroiled and then locked in a near-endless match, neither man wanting to relinquish the reward he can see for his efforts. Both men do indeed serve big, backing it up with their solid and concise grass court games and there are few breaks of serve over the five sets. For these two men, it is a once-in-a-lifetime opportunity. The balance between the two players is on a knife-edge, is there for the taking, is going to be decided over the next hour or so. Someone needs to break serve, but they have both been broken at least once in each of the last two sets. This is one of those occasions when either player losing seems a harsh outcome. But there are no draws here. It must be decided, it is clinical, and someone will be left to rue the day, soaked in salty regret and the sweat of the battle.

It is the longest semi-final in Wimbledon history when, finally, it ends – perhaps another unwanted record for today's defeated player, American John Isner. It stretched from lunch to dinner, and beyond, as the two tall figures played on. Anderson prevails 7-6, 6-7, 6-7, 6-4, 26-24, but, well, what will he have left in his tank for the biggest match of his career only two days later?

On the flip side of the semi-final coin...

Not since the 2011 Men's Wimbledon final have these two greats of the sport met on the lawns of Wimbledon's Centre Court (or any other court at SW19). But today, after the Kevin Anderson and John Isner semi-final (when it eventually finished), Novak Djokovic took on Rafael Nadal for a place in the final. The two greats of modern tennis hold five Wimbledon titles between them (Novak with three, and Rafa with two).

Just after 11pm and the action finally concludes for the day – yet unfinished – with Djokovic having just taken the third set tie-break over Nadal, for a two-sets-to-one lead overnight. The tie-break, as with many of their amazing classics in the past decade, came down to one or two points – mistakes, slight errors of judgement and decision making – and Nadal is left to repent for his on-court shortcomings, to sleep on a pillow of his own dissatisfaction.

When the Men Invaded Ladies' Final Day

Maybe the weirdest Wimbledon fortnight on record. Granted, I haven't seen all the Championships, but separating this from others has been the top ten ladies' seeds all falling by the close of play on the second Monday, the huge favourite in the men's draw losing in the quarter-final (after being two sets to love up), then the longest semi-final in Wimbledon history – lasting over six and a half hours – before the other two men played out their own classic encounter (yet again!).

The culmination of the second men's semi-final took place prior to the women's singles final, making it anything but a traditional Centre Court spectacle on the second Saturday. And the final tasted different after seeing Nadal finally succumb to Djokovic's recovered invincibility.

Angie puts Serena to the sword and gains revenge for her loss at this same stage two years before. Kerber also grabs her third Grand Slam title (and third different one, now only missing the Roland Garros title for a full set) and returns to some of the form we saw in 2016. It's a wonderful accomplishment. Serena will have to wait, but for now, it's great to see she is putting herself in the position to find major title number 24.

I Told Novak Djokovic to Play Wimbledon

I'm not saying he listened, or that he even heard my ticking thoughts documented on Twitter. Maybe my tweet never reached his eyes (it would be lost amidst the sea of online drivel spouted daily), and maybe he didn't base a decision – about not skipping the grass court season, as he had previously indicated as a viable option – around my words of encouragement post his Roland Garros quarter-final exit less than six weeks earlier. But I'd seen all I needed to, to know the Serbian wizard was back to casting his greatest spells on opponents as he had up until 2016. So, yes, I told Novak Djokovic to play Wimbledon. I told him in a tweet, publicly so, and I told him he would win the event, knowing that, of course, King Roger was nigh on everyone's favourite, defending his title as he was. My window into the future had shown me the eventual outcome as Novak once again claimed the ultimate prize, holding aloft the golden trophy for a fourth time

Maybe Djokovic had had no real intention of missing Wimbledon, as he had stated in the aftermath to the clay court season's close. However, he was obviously where he needed to be to win it, and that *could* be seen during the French Open only weeks before, despite his loss to Marco Cecchinato there, and how badly he took that. Don't be surprised if he is unplayable and therefore unbeatable again, very, very soon. Wimbledon is just the start of a brand new chapter for the Serbian legend.

The Algorithm of Tennis

The swings and roundabouts, the great carousel of sport. History echoes, and new versions stand before us. Like a language, tennis follows formats and patterns, computed messages that those who speak fluently can predict, can comment upon, can bask in. Looking deeply enough, they (the recognisable graph lines) reveal themselves over time in a variety of ways.

Matches have multiple permutations and yet, despite always having their own original identity, it often feels that 'we've been here before', that something akin to this has been previously lived. Trends are recognised and matches fit into columns of contest-type, match-up, or performance. While no two matches, or moments in life, are ever identical, there is a prevalent sense when watching sport and tennis that patterns are emerging, that it isn't an authentic sequence of events.

And how could it be? When watching a lot of anything, similarities will arise and surprises will be few and far between. The algorithm of tennis is familiar; sequences become clear. There are no draws, no saving one's best for another day without ruing that choice. It is one or the other. It is close, or it is not. Each set offers the potential for its own war; sometimes sets reflect a switch in fortunes and players' grooves, crowds are invested, indifferent, biased, well-balanced and so on. While there are many factors to take into consideration, it is rare that a new factor or mood will have anything to do with a tried and tested, known algorithm.

Looking into a future window, I knew the pattern when Petra Kvitová started to pull away from Belinda Bencic in the second set of the Dubai Championships final in

February 2019. I knew Petra would win the second set to level the match and that the momentum she had gathered would then likely be ended early in set three. Which it was. The shift would then take place and it was likely, albeit not certain, that Bencic would go on to win the match.

Bencic does win. I feel like I have seen it before, and yet, I have not. Much like a Rubik's Cube, there are a limited number of possibilities. While tennis is affected by almost endless forces, the outcomes are restricted to a win or a loss for either player involved. Then, a win or loss could be in straight sets or it could go to a deciding set; a shift in momentum witnessed before the early end that a straight sets victory sees. Each point is a question of rhythm, tactics, luck, confidence, energy, crowd support, mood and the weather conditions on any given day. Ability comes into it, but does not always stamp its master print upon events.

And so, while no two faces are the same, you often feel that you've seen one before or that someone closely resembles another person, and such is the case with tennis matches. Each has its twin or triplet whilst being wholly unique. There emerge the patterns that define the sport, that render us rarely able to witness something truly new, and which provide a reassurance in sport that comforts us in our viewing.

Ultimately, tennis is anything but predictable – ask anyone who has suffered the failure to convert match points and gone on to lose a match. Tennis is about sealing the deal; you can be so close and yet so very far. There are enough permutations in tennis, as well as constant changes to the game, characters to love and loathe and exterior factors that shape matches, conditions and player responses, to ensure it is never anything but boring.

PARTY
HARD

Tears of Reason or an Open Letter to Andy Murray

3rd August 2018

Dear Andy Murray, or Sir,

if ever the emergence of tears made sense and provided the perfect ending to another marathon tussle in Washington (that's three in a row), then this was it, this was their chance to glisten and shine. Hidden as they were by a towel over your face, nothing could hide the fact that you were sobbing into your towel at the achievement, at your return after a year (at this level), and perhaps even surprised by your own guts to deliver so soon after that much time side-lined through injury. The not knowing whether you could ever climb back, if you'd ever be able to compete, to match the obstacles put in front of you – the mental, the physical, the everything. The world kept turning in your absence. Maybe you felt it was leaving you behind.

This was something special. It could be felt, by all those invested in tennis – the players, the fans, the officials and media – that this was a grand moment. A shaking of the shoulders, an audible sob of broken joy and disbelief; the horror, the release, the cathartic expression of all that pain.

For sharing yourself, your very being, with us, unreservedly, and for what you bring to tennis, thank you kindly,

Dominic J Stevenson

The Greek God of Tennis is but a Teenager

That Stefanos Tsitsipas' favourite surface is grass proves just how far he has come. His clay court exploits earlier in the season, and his now increasingly impressive results in the early stages of the latest hard-court season, have earmarked him as one for the future of men's tennis. The future seems to be coming into view much sooner than anticipated and the Greeks have a genuine no-filler god on their hands, as does the wider world of tennis. Yesterday's victory over recent Wimbledon champion and returned top tenner, Novak Djokovic, at the Rogers Cup, should see Tsitsipas climb to a career-high ranking next week yet again. His current ranking post of 27 marks a startling ascendency over recent months, turning 2018 into his undeniable breakthrough year. At only 19, he is one of the few players who looks like an authentic challenger to Alexander Zverev over the coming decade.

Andrey Rublev and Hyeon Chung, two of the most impressive young players of 2017 and of the first edition of the NextGen tournament last year, have been blighted with injury throughout this year – and have missed a substantial opportunity to kick on from some brilliant 2017/early 2018 scenes. Denis Shapovalov, also 19, has pressed on, and along with Tsitsipas, looks like the other rightful heir to the throne of men's tennis. Others who can carve impressive results, but perhaps not quite as consistently, are Borna Ćorić, Daniil Medvedev, Taylor Fritz and Alex de Minaur.

My other favourite youngster is 20-year old Frances Tiafoe. He narrowly missed out against Grigor Dimitrov yesterday in a tight third set. Experience was, seemingly,

31

the deciding factor. This week, only Tsitsipas is left standing, with his quarter-final berth seeing him once again face Alexander Zverev, who dispatched him in rather a straightforward manner last week in Washington (the German, Zverev, went on to defend his title there).

I wouldn't be surprised if today's match is more of a contest. The young Greek has already overcome Damir Džumhur, Dominic Thiem and Djokovic (two top ten players in the last two rounds) in the first three rounds of this year's Rogers Cup, and will fear nobody. That he is improving with every tournament – even every match he plays – evokes the fluidity, grace and efficiency of Roger Federer, at times, more than any other young player. He has already pieced together the tour and its intricate workings, at such a tender age, and this makes him a remarkably gifted and appealing prospect. Undeniably, his potential is almost endless. He looks like the 2018 incarnation of Björn Borg, he wears his heart on his sleeve, and more than any other aspect, he *knows* he is good enough, now, to challenge and push the world's best players. This week proves that, and backs up his previous results this season. When you start putting together a run like this, it is no fluke. Soon the world's top 20 will include him and Denis Shapovalov. Then, there is no looking back, and surely, it's just a matter of time until these two names join Zverev in the top ten and then the top five.

The men's game hasn't changed for a long time, but it is finally happening.

Don't be surprised if Rafael Nadal and Federer, and maybe even Djokovic too, are soon edged out of the running for the big titles. These kids are as hungry as they are, and Tsitsipas is just what tennis has been needing – a breath of fresh air, a Greek god with just the image to launch a thousand advertising campaigns, and break a million hearts every time he loses. More than any of that, what beautiful tennis the young man plays. What absolutely beautiful tennis he plays. Make no mistake, this young player is here to stay.

Scheduling Mess

Your scheduling is a mess. Rounds commenced long before others have finished, players having to play two matches a day to keep on track... and all because of a little rain.

Spare a thought for Aryna Sabalenka, the Belarussian, who yesterday came back from a set down against the reigning Australian Open champion and world number two, Caroline Wozniacki. The smile on her face told its tale in the immediate aftermath of the biggest win of her career. That she had to return the same day, after such exploits, and again play a tough three-set match against Elise Mertens – this time, sadly, and hardly unexpectedly, on the losing side – seems almost unfathomable. She played one set more than the men who must go all the way to five sets in a Grand Slam match.

Having beaten Wozniacki, who hadn't hit a ball in the competition until their second-round encounter on Thursday, she had to return to court only 90 minutes later. Yes, it sometimes happens, yes. Perhaps on occasion it is even unavoidable. But more needs to be done to protect players and escape such situations as this. There's every possibility that with appropriate and fair recovery time, Sabalenka would have made her way past Elise Mertens and into the last eight later today. It happened to Andy Murray last week in Washington, in a slightly different scenario, where he was also required to play an inhumane amount of tennis across a short period of time, having only just returned from a serious injury. Indeed, he had to pull out and say 'no more!' He is not one to shirk his responsibilities as a player but, as with Sabalenka, too much is being asked of these players at times. They are being put last: after the events, and the fans, and the revenues they bring in. Not to mention that naughty force of nature known as the weather. Without the players there is NO tennis. They should be put first, protected, and valued.

Sort this palaver out. Aryna Sabalenka should never be playing six sets in a day. Andy Murray should never be playing three consecutive three-set matches (in three days), late at night, with no time for recovery. I understand these tournaments are affected by inclement weather and that late finishes sometimes occur, but *use the other courts*, and make sure no round is started before the previous one is finished. It shows the players that they are the key ingredient in all of this.

Another Poor Zverev Racket Bites the Dust

Smashing a racket can release the tension. That killer expression of fury, frustration, and inner fire. It can hardly be viewed as the most acceptable outlet, however, most often seeming like the brattiest thing to do – like a baby throwing its dummy out of the pram. But there are times when it becomes a mechanical and poor – rather pathetic even – ritual that denies personal expansion and reflects the absence of a coping mechanism regarding losing sets and matches.

No sportsperson can get through a tennis career without a good experience of both victory and loss. Alexander Zverev, however – as talented as he may be – is not impervious to such loss. His strange swagger, potentially viewed as a ballooned ego worn as a badge, possibly alienates the humbler and equally hard-working players amongst his peers. For he does have failures. And he has more by the day. As Stefanos Tsitsipas has just moments earlier proven, by winning the second set in a marathon tie-break – 13-11 – against the German.

It's a match – the pair's Rogers Cup quarter-final – that the young Greek goes on to win, dispatching Zverev 6-4 in the third and decisive set, leaving the average tennis fan left wondering a) how good is Tsitsipas, and b) where is it presently going wrong with the young Zverev? He certainly needs to change something, bring in the right people, and rectify the matter regarding his recent failure to match the expectations he and others have placed on his shoulders. Perhaps the heavy burden surrounding him, and since such a young age, is exactly what is causing these problems? On the other hand, he may be very close to banishing these troubles and becoming the player he's looked set to become. Either way, the saga continues, and the rackets, unfortunately, continue to meet their makers.

Halep v Stephens
(Rogers Cup Final)

In a rematch of this year's Roland Garros final, the ladies' showpiece finds Simona Halep facing off against Sloane Stephens. Stephens, further cementing her remarkable ascendency to the upper echelons of the tennis mountain, begins to look unbeatable at certain stages of this final.

As the first set tie-break reaches 6-6, and the players change ends, it seems there is a ghost in the machine of each player's game. There have been moments of brilliance followed quickly by frustration, mistakes, and lost opportunities. And the set goes on. Neither player wanting to fall, neither thus far executing the pearl-like chance to claim the opener. Until Halep finds a way, as she often does, to take it 8-6 in the tie-break. She saved four set points in the process. Now, *that* is grit and determination.

Stephens then pushes her way into a final set, forcing the Halep hand, by winning 6-3 in the second. Halep, then, as is becoming something of a routine, remains with her opponent, only to find a way to pull away and win the match, 6-4 in the third and final set, with the decisive venom doing its sometime trick. She echoes her victory in Paris, in another tight encounter with Stephens. Stephens every inch the rival now, a challenger through and through, shades of someone with her eyes on further Slams and the number one ranking. For now, Halep looks the part.

And over in the men's Rogers Cup final, Rafael Nadal gives Stefanos Tsitsipas his second and latest lesson, on the young Greek's 20th birthday, making the champions in Canada the same as the ones in this year's second Grand Slam in Paris. While, notably on different surfaces, it demonstrates perhaps why they are the world number ones

– and they both have some very impressive form to take in to Flushing Meadows in New York two weeks from now (the final major of 2018).

If the Net Could Speak...

If the net could speak, well, what would it say? About its close calls with players hurtling towards it? Its observations of balls like missiles – flying just over, smacking into, or clipping? Or its decisions on which side to let the fuzzy yellow ones drop?

The net, always in the middle of everything, would have some stories to tell: far-fetched and fascinating, an encyclopaedia of the sport.

The (occasional) newly-implemented netcam is a device that lends a further perspective; something I had been longing for as a tennis fan. It adds another understanding to the visual translation of what happens on court, a dimension that has lacked in past incarnations of the sport. It's only in use at some events, and perhaps it is in its infancy with regard to television coverage, but it has great potential to add a fresh view to what has been transmitted in a tried and tested format for a long time now. Change, evolution, and the expansion of our sport can only be a good thing, I hear you say. Depending on the adaptations, indeed.

FANFARE AT FLUSHING MEADOWS

The Halep Hiccup /
The David Ferrer Blues

Following – not to mention supporting – Simona Halep has become a journey of unexpected adventures. She entered the US Open with some exceptional form, with a recent trophy and runners up medal at the Rogers Cup and Cincinnati events respectively. To see her plummet into the early round loss abyss on day one was another strange stumble. Just when you think you heard a 'click' of it all falling into place, her functionality fails and her humanity is revealed. She often doesn't get going in the early rounds, but somehow finds a way through. This time no such luck, as Estonia's Kaia Kanepi addressed the match-up with the ultimate aggressive mindset; it didn't allow Halep to settle or feel comfortable for even a moment. Halep was not joined by the other top seeds today, marking her exit as the main drama of the day.

The legendary Spanish stalwart, David Ferrer, took his Grand Slam bow last night. Not quite in the manner he would have chosen to see out his first-round encounter against world number one, reigning champion, and compatriot Rafael Nadal, but it did show his characteristic grit and passion for the sport, not to mention his humble humanity. It would be remiss of me if I did not state, in no uncertain terms, that David Ferrer will be missed. While never climbing to the Grand Slam heights that the three key players of the era have, and not even having managed a single Slam title as a small handful of others have, he has been close on several occasions and has shown a zest and fight and spirit that few others can claim to have. He epitomises the never-say-die Spanish sporting mentality of nowadays. He has been one of the leading figures of the sport in Spain, and beyond, over the last decade and his unfortunate exit last night – at the hands of injury – halfway through the second set, level on serve, and only a set down, seems symbolic of why he needs to call it a day. His raging inferno within remains, his desire to play is unquestionable, but his body – slowing and breaking down – is having the final say.

Ferrer has played some remarkable matches over the years. For me, his Davis Cup victory over Philipp Kohlschreiber earlier this year, was one of his crowning moments, taking place in front of many of his family and friends as it did. Played out in his back garden in Valencia, it showed why he has been such a special and important player, his humanity and tennis character laid bare. He is – along with Rafa – the ultimate sporting and tennis role model. A trooper who never gave up. Some of the young brats of today could already learn greatly from him and his work.

Battle of the Younglings
(Medvedev v Tsitsipas)

Daniil Medvedev, hot on the heels of winning in Winston-Salem last week, is looking rather lethal as he tears ahead into a set and a break lead over recent on-court wizard and wunderkind Stefanos Tsitsipas in their second round encounter at this year's US Open.

Medvedev has looked good for some time now, and whilst perhaps not of the ilk of a Zverev Jr or a Shapovalov (and, well, let's watch all their progress closely), on his day he is a massive test for many of the players on the ATP tour.

With the confidence gained last week, with the ability he clearly possesses, Tsitsipas' own form and confidence might well take a beating here, as the Russian pushes into some inspired terrain. Either way, we are in for a spectacle, as Medvedev moves closer to closing out the second set, for a substantial lead. He takes it. He then lets Tsitsipas back in by losing set three, until returning to his peerless pop of the first two sets. It is the Russian who seizes his third-round berth, and lodges another good win under his belt, marking himself as one to watch, now and further down the line.

Elsewhere, Victoria Azarenka was pinning number 25 seed Daria Gavrilova to the post, finishing her off with sublime ease. Don't say she's back, don't even whisper it, as she has been growing in stature for some time now. But the Belarusian mother looks rather good indeed. Watch this space for more on her exploits.

Sabalenka Goes One Way, Millman the Other

Sabalenka looks deadly. Then loses. There is great magic there, the power and the beauty, and the ugliness of modern tennis. Love her, like her, loathe her, she is here to stay and will find herself – if things progress as they seem to be – very near the top of women's tennis at a stadium near you. *Coming soon.* Surely.

Day eight witnesses the shock of the season – Roger Federer loses, failing to make his projected quarter-final date with Novak Djokovic in two days' time.

I don't know any other sport in which you have to play your opponent and the entire crowd. Maybe boxing in the country of an opposition fighter. But silence isn't necessary in boxing and the behaviour of some fans towards the magnificent victor of the hour – Australia's John Millman – is anything but appropriate/respectful/gracious. Many are glory hunters, hoping Federer's Uniqlo outfit will get snagged on their pawing fingers, so they get taken along for the ride. John Millman was exceptional and deserves an immense ovation. That is what sport is. Not one man, not one force that is greater than all. Roger Federer's career has been a revelation, and I cannot add much to the overspill of words about his greatness on this occasion, especially as I reside in the camp of other players, regardless of Grand Slam wins. So, to hear fans cheering and applauding Millman missing his serves in the final stages of the match, was both unwarranted and entirely disrespectful to the sport, not to mention the man himself. This is not restricted to the current location; it goes far beyond, but it does seem to have a field day in some settings. Cheering failures and mistakes is a spectacular weight to cope with. Millman seemingly shrugged off the bad behaviour, was understated in his victorious moment, and class that should be remembered.

And with the Twitterverse (and beyond) stunned, with Federer's dejected body language and sweat pouring off him – yes, you've read that right; a seldom seen sight – it became clear that the conditions (as well as a wily Australian fox) had got the better of him this time.

Ladies' Singles Final
Serena Williams v Naomi Osaka

Serena Williams spectacularly implodes. For everything she has done both in and for the game – for women and equality – she is wholly questionable today; she is damaging to the sport (and perhaps even wider society). As she launches into several tirades at an umpire simply applying the rules to a tennis match. As she uses her status as a mother, almost holding up a photo of her little daughter to justify her ugly words and the manner in which she viciously launches them with the whole world watching on, completely convinced that she is in the right and everyone else not in agreement with her is anything but. As she stops the flow of the match, effortlessly spoiling the occasion and somehow not halting the charge of her young opponent, Naomi Osaka. Today is meant to be about the winner. Alas, today it is not so.

In nearly 30 years of watching tennis, I have never witnessed anything like this before — a player receiving their first Grand Slam trophy and looking heartbroken with tears dried on her cheeks. The crowd confusingly boo and jeer until Queen Serena tells them to cool it in the aftermath of the madness. The issues of nationalism and fanaticism, blinding people to unacceptable social behaviour, are unavoidable at such a time. We should all be swallowing the pill of delight at having another new young major winner amongst us, and yet we are not, and social media will take its fine-tooth comb and rip this final and the post-details apart. People will apply extreme bias and beliefs to these events, making things acceptable that should not be in any avenue of life. There are channels to complain and express dissatisfaction through. This is not the correct stage, not the time, nor the place.

Nothing is ever truly simple. No one angle or view, but a multifaceted array of opinions and arguments. This one seemingly has two chief sides. Right and wrong. Good and bad. Rules and respect against standing up for oneself.

The emotion of the day, of the occasion, of it all. There is a time and a place for such an overflowing of emotion. This was not it. This is entirely how this ladies' final will be remembered, and that is unfortunate indeed.

Men's Singles Final
Novak Djokovic v
Juan Martin del Potro

Juan Martin del Potro has had an amazing tournament, but nobody beats Novak Djokovic when he is in this mood, this hungry. The Djokovic tantrums, when he started to struggle with Delpo briefly, were the diva we all know emerging; it would be nice to see him learning to accept those moments with a little more humility as players often do. But, the diva, as many times before, only served to aid him, whip and scold him, unlike Serena's diva of the night before.

It's hard, at times, based on the behaviour, not to contemplate how much money these sportspeople make and already have. It is not that they do not deserve it. Not at all. They have dedicated a huge part of their lives to reaching the level of success they attain. When it comes down to it, is *that* what we want to be considering when we follow and watch sport closely and lovingly – how rich they are? One's on-court behaviour reflects what is socially acceptable. At times, you get the feeling it just doesn't mean that much to some of these top sporting figures to be such powerful role models.

Djokovic is back to his best, another Grand Slam title to add to his tally, which now totals 14.

Del Potro, whilst obviously feeling a little disappointed, might well be thrilled to be back in a final of such note, close to another major glory, and keeping those pesky injuries at bay. A final to remember, for the right reasons.

The Other Fifty Weeks

As with the mechanism of a clock, the greatest part and its intricacies go unseen; almost nothing visible to those observing it. Imagining what it takes to put a Grand Slam tournament together over the entire year might just lend a similar perspective. An incredible amount of work is undertaken, all year round, to hosting these enormous events; they rarely fail to wow the public present, and those watching from elsewhere in the tennis stratosphere. The fluid mechanics in place keep things ticking over just nicely.

When we think of the big tournaments, we reminisce about our key memories, filled with nostalgia as we are. We picture the faces and the glory painted thereon, the exquisite pain and heartbreak, no middle ground ever recalled. We have our favourite events and moments of the calendar year, and we see little, if anything, of the sheer volume of work that goes into those beloved tournaments, all year round, in order to prepare for the following year's edition, and with the hope that it gets somewhat better each time. Members of staff – the hidden teams tasked with providing the hungry tennis public with enough brilliant action to sate their appetites – work like ants behind the scenes preparing every aspect of what, for two weeks, becomes something of a town, with a colossal influx, with a great drain on resources, as people eat and drink and use other facilities, and generally demand a perfect experience.

Not to mention the intense and almost interminable hard work and training and plotting and scheming that goes into the players' assaults on the big-time events. Offensives that bring the key glory, money, records, and limelight.

Life is full of hidden treasures, mechanisms that hold great value and which are perhaps underestimated, if appreciated at all. No sooner has the curtain has fallen on another fortnight of tennis magic than the work that never stops turns to preparation for the following year's tournament. Thousands of faces lodged in the walls of a major tennis competition go about their roles on-site, working at improving and building something, a crescendo that ends in an explosive fortnight of hundreds and hundreds of tennis matches.

The Umpire-Verbal-Assault-Volley That Shall Not Be Named

Not the kind of volley we are looking for; not as tennis spectators, not as umpires, not as other players and coaches. Occasionally, something occurs with such great impact that a near-cacophony of endless voices – all jostling to be heard – emerge from behind cyber walls, volcanic in their effect. A polemic discussion not done with being reasonable in mind.

Serena Williams' brutal verbal assault on Carlos Ramos was matched with widespread anger and widespread support. Rules were broken, those same rules were followed, punishment implemented, and the effects sent waves. However, from a perspective of protection, rules exist for a reason. If every player out there pushes the rules (or not), and gets away with things (or not), if the rules – when applied – favour or denounce players over others, it is simply part and parcel of the tennis life, as are rules to life in general. As with any sport, what is questionable, is how consistent the application of the rules enforced across the board is. There is room for improvement; some umpires are more lenient than others, bringing their own characters to the occasions. Carlos Ramos is a fine umpire with a fantastic history. It's a shame he had to be made a scapegoat, and that the spotlight shone upon him was so unnecessary. We should refer to this in future as 'the umpire-verbal-assault-volley that shall not be named'.

Players who have elevated themselves – with help of media and mass numbers of spectators and fans – above the laws of the lawns and courts, well, that remains with those individuals. If sexism exists in the game, it didn't appear to on that day. That's a much wider scope and a totally different discussion for another time.

Using one's status as a parent, or a warrior, or any other vulnerable or all-powerful entity is not something that denotes elegance or eloquence at accepting one's fate with humility and grace. Granted, those features are not ones that define everyone, maybe not even most, but on and off the court, would life not be easier if people abided by general rules and didn't cast such toxic assumptions so freely? Social media, clearly, aids and abets that design, as people club one another invisibly, a little like tennis players battering balls at one another, only with malice and anger in mind. The effects are hurtful, harming more than can be known, cultivating further damage to wider society.

...And with The Djokovic Return Complete

Without a shadow of a doubt, Novak Djokovic will imminently be crowned world number one again – for the fourth time. Nobody can deny it is both merited and has been coming.

He's in the kind of form – yes, *that* kind – that perhaps only he has ever truly displayed. On occasion, Rafael Nadal or Roger Federer could remain with him, maybe even outlast him, but it cannot be understated that he has a winning record against both men – the two everyone continues to argue over who might be the Greatest Of All Time. He is now the only one, ever, to have won all nine Masters Tournaments. He has all the Grand Slams under his belt, the year-end tournament he has also claimed on multiple occasions. What else?

I recently saw someone on social media question how, in the men's game, you could possibly win the last two Grand Slam titles and still not be the world number one. The annual tennis calendar, however, that contributes to both ranking and the ATP and WTA races to the year-end events, runs over the course of the year, not half a season. Djokovic had a slow start to the year, and since the mid-way mark has become nigh-on unstoppable. Therefore, the world number one – Nadal – is about to be replaced by the highly successful recent figure in question; his own Serbian nemesis of sorts, Djokovic. Form over the last ten months is what contributes to the now imminent year-end number one ranking, and not four months. That is how it is determined.

The WTA Finals Are Go!

The eight best female players of the year – with the exception of year-end number one Simona Halep (replaced by Dutch lady Kiki Bertens, who had her finest year by far to date) – line up in Singapore, gearing up for glory, one last precious prize for another season, as its flame is ready to be snuffed out.

Kiki Bertens is the fortunate one – benefitting from Halep's withdrawal due to a back injury – so, the 2nd to the 9th best players in the world are the final field here. Somehow, as a heading, as a lead line, it doesn't quite have the same ring to it. Nevertheless, it's a quality field, and fans of women's tennis all have their eyes fixed towards the court in Singapore in anticipation of who might prevail. A case could be made for each of the octet. With three of the four Grand Slam winners from this past season – in Caroline Wozniacki, Angelique Kerber and Naomi Osaka – plus the now perennially impressive and reliable Elina Svitolina, plus Sloane Stephens, Petra Kvitová, Karolina Plíšková and the aforementioned Kiki Bertens, it is an electrifying prospect.

Each player has *earned* their place in this last eight.

At the gala photo shoot (a thing of habit each year) the women are snapped from multiple angles in dresses and make up that let's face it, isn't how we normally see these icons (the men similarly wear suits at the ATP equivalent event).

Wozniacki is defending her title, but Osaka might be viewed as the one to beat in the aftermath of her US Open win and ranking ascent and, frankly, any of the other six women listed above could be dangerous should they find their feet in the group phase which wonderfully launches players into the final stages of the year's closing event. Momentum is ever the valuable commodity to sportspeople the world over.

Tussle

It was hardly surprising, given the standings before this match commenced, that the Elina Svitolina and Caroline Wozniacki pairing spawned arguably the match of the group phase so far. A semi-final berth was on the line with Karolína Plíšková having earlier booked her own place in the next stage by defeating Petra Kvitová (herself being subjected to a third straight defeat on her way tumbling out).

At the midway stage in the final set, Svitolina seems to be in the ascendency. It doesn't matter that she narrowly lost the first set 7-5. Nor that she reversed that scoreline in the second set. What matters is the third and final set, a shoot-out, as it is often referred to, in what is proving to be an epic tussle.

Svitolina just needs to serve out the match. No straightforward task, given Wozniacki's ability to turn potential defeat into victory on a great number of occasions. In fact, along with Simona Halep, she has possibly been the best at this, over recent years. And as Svitolina gives her a lifeline, Wozniacki gets to 0-40 on her opponent's serve; it looks like this match isn't over yet.

Then, 15-40... 30-40... one more chance for the break, right now... and deuce. Wozniacki crunches a return into the net. Svitolina, having saved three break-back points, late in the day, has a match point.

Denied.

The tussle continues. Back to deuce. The WTA is rich, indeed. Wozniacki with yet another breakpoint, but again her shot meets the net, and another chance is gone. They are there; the failure to seize them will soon be the abiding memory of the match. This time Svitolina reaches advantage and finally wins the match on a sliced drop shot to end a rally that used the whole court. During the exchange, Wozniacki offered a weak smash that Svitolina tentatively got back in court. Chances like that will be rued. The reigning champion is out, her Ukrainian White Group conqueror progresses, having won all three of her group matches. Svitolina will be hard to beat this week. Wozniacki will be disappointed, but when she looks back on the year, it's the one that stands out the most so far.

Hurtling Balls

The ball comes hurtling through the air, losing speed, but meeting the body of the boards behind, before anyone notices the pace dropping off. It's another winner from a devilish racket, smacking them all over for fun, from seemingly anywhere on the court, even from way outside both the tramlines and the back of the court. The little yellow hairs of the ball are being torn asunder as each ball is pulverised repeatedly.

That Double Fault

Yes, that one. That double fault. Federer, 3-1 down in the final set tie-break of a marathon three-setter in the Paris Masters semi-final, having not double-faulted in the whole match. He introduces the unwanted and gifts Djokovic a 4-1 lead, that of course a player of such calibre would not relinquish. The lead impossible to overcome, the Serbian would then cruise further ahead, as it became 5-1 at the change of ends.

That double fault showed the great master as human, which, let's face it, after three hours of play of that quality, given his age, doesn't really seem believable. It is possible, though, and it's to acknowledge and credit Federer that he is still able to play at this level. What is clear is that his two decades of tennis, which have easily defined him as the most elegant and perfectly-formed tennis player ever, are a once-in-a-lifetime case. Many who have gone before have long since hung up their rackets, gone into hiding, into commentary booths, into coaching roles and court-side team boxes, and so on and so forth. None have made it to such a standard at a similar age.

At this stage, that double fault would prove the difference after Djokovic's successful next two service points, between being 5-2 down, a glimmer of hope, or being 6-1 down and facing five match points. An irretrievable match when playing against the brutal Novak Djokovic. That double fault was epic, somehow deeply telling, and fatal. After all that hard work, having given himself a shot, having worked himself into the match-end equation.

It's hard to argue that what had come before – over a gruelling indoor hard-court match – was not one of the matches of the year: a clear highlight, a testament to this match-up. Who knows how many more times these players will meet, but for now, everything about the pairing is to be enjoyed, whatever the specific outcome may be. Djokovic goes on to meet first-timer Karen Khachanov in the final, but the level of Federer – just as the shots he plays – is genuinely still a thing of wonder.

Edition Two of the NextGen ATP Finals

The field of eight includes seven thoroughly deserved participants who are under-21, and one lucky qualifier. Based on their exploits over the season that started in January, much as with the final line-up for the ATP Finals in London, there is no argument that these spots have been earned. The final spot is awarded to an Italian player who comes through a qualifying event in Milan prior to the five-day event each year.

New and old fans, alike, are chomping at the bit to witness the young future stars pulverising that ball at one another. While it is nice to hand out a spot to a qualifier of the event's home country, it does feel something of a slight to the player who finishes eighth each year in the official ATP Race to Milan. This year, for example, the Italian qualifier inclusion is ranked outside the world's top 600, while the remainder are in the top 100. An exciting opportunity also means a small imbalance in the line-up.

There are moments when this event is labelled, and touted, as the future of tennis. A sport that has maintained many of its traditions and sequences for the best part of a century scarcely needs such revolution, and while all must have their day – handing over the baton and evolving – many of these changes simply wouldn't improve general events and tennis tours. It does offer some bright new possibilities – such as the towel rack, which sends players to retrieve their own towels, and the medical time-outs – that much is true, but the existing template should more or less be left as it is. Tampering with the rules regarding coaching during matches, shorter warm-ups, and no-let rules, not to mention the length of the sets, is needless, for anything other than the spectacle of this event. If taken for what it is, Next Gen is a bright new event, still evolving. If taken as a measuring stick for the future of the sport, that has held itself so well for so long, it'd be a travesty to change and ruin it for good. Just look at the death of the Davis Cup, a passing that has devastated many amongst the tennis community. What it is being replaced with is a cynical money-spinning exercise.

Next Gen ATP Final

This year's tournament has not only shown how the youngsters of the time are exceptionally gifted, but it has showcased them as a field of 'never-say-die' on-court warriors. Perhaps just a first point of contact for some fans with Alex de Minaur, Jaume Munar, Hubert Hurkacz, and Taylor Fritz – these players have all left a good account of their on-court characters. It cannot be underestimated how long the season is, though, and how this 'NextGen' showcase at its end might not find the young men in the most fresh and dynamic states.

As we enter a tie-break shootout for the third set – at one set all – some of the tennis played by both Stefanos Tsitsipas and Alex de Minaur has been as inspirational and stunning as people might have hoped the final of this new annual fixture would be. In a heavenly unfolding scenario, the teenage Aussie, de Minaur, and the 20-year-old Greek, Tsitsipas, have shown not only their wonderful range of skills and armour but underscored how they have been two of the finest players of the year in all of men's tennis.

Their respective climbs up the rankings since the outset of 2018 have both been epic – de Minaur rising from 208 to 31, and Tsitsipas from 91 to 15. Their ascents represent their improvements (and the early stage at which they are able to make them), their potential, and their undeniable ability to face challenges head-on, on the biggest stages of the sport. Here are two players with the correct tennis genes to go a long way. This year was just the infancy of their big match careers. These players shared just six ATP match wins between them before January 2018. Not even two handfuls. Now they have over 70 wins between them just in 2018. The rise may not be complete, but you certainly cannot fluke such outcomes.

2019 should see the top 10 inhale both players into its midst (or thereabouts), where, when they do finally get there, we can expect – barring any serious injuries – both players to reside for a great many years. This is no NextGen; rankings do not lie. These two players mark their names as a couple that could do some serious damage next year, under spotlights, at major tennis events the globe over.

De Minaur, wise, calm, and skilful beyond his years, looks capable of anything. His growth and maturity are magical to observe; a young man with a deeply warm character and a focus, which are both highly admirable at his age. His Greek opponent today could surely enter the ATP top ten by the spring should he get a good start to 2019 and continue his rapid rise to the top of the game. He proves too much on this occasion for De Minaur, winning 2-4, 4-1, 4-3, 4-3.

Alexander Zverev will know these two are coming. He will know that Federer, Nadal, and Djokovic's eventual retirements will not make anything easier as he takes his own focused aim on hitting the ultimate heights of the sport.

This era, comprising the last decade and a half – has included three of the greatest male tennis players ever. It may be coming to a close, but there will be no easy wins at majors. There is about to be an even greater number of possible winners at that level, as Khachanov, Ćorić, Chung, Medvedev, Zverev, Tsitsipas, de Minaur, Shapovalov, Tiafoe, Fritz, Rublev, Munar and a great many others join the fore.

Stefanos Tsitsipas is, of course, a thoroughly deserved – and possibly slightly predictable - winner of the Next Gen tournament by the end of the week. He's had a year that puts him head and shoulders above the other competitors. Who knows what comes next for one of the players of 2018.

Father Federer

Roger Federer is not old, and, in addition, time has been kind to him. Redefining its parameters, however, to elongate an already breathtaking career, is seemingly all that's on his mind – giving himself a chance at further building on his existing legacy. No desire to (or sign of) quit when further records remain to be broken. He wants to install himself deeper in the record books that are unlikely to be re-written any time soon, if ever, after his accomplishments. Time is indeed lending him its hour, minute, and second hands.

At gone 37, he is still better than most, still dispatching opponents who are well over ten years his junior. Approximately 20 years in the game (as a professional), it's hard to predict when he wants to quit. More than at any specific age, it's likely it will be when the wheels slow, and he can no longer beat players he currently beats. While he is winning matches – and how – he doesn't look invincible as he did in 2017. Not at all. Reputation and fear from his opponents are certainly carrying him a distance, too, of late. But who can picture the great Federer losing in early rounds to inferior players, accepting a sliding ranking, and placing a shadow over his reputation? He will know. I think we all will. And he will be sorely missed.

The future of an entire sport, however, goes on. It will go on, and it'll be richer for having had Federer and his few true peers grace the planet's courts. What we should all remember – especially the glory-hunters amongst us – is that no one player or team is ever bigger than a sport. While it may be individuals who draw the observers – a multitude of global fans to the sport – without that beautiful game nobody would be watching in the first place.

The grand old man of tennis – the elder statesman and player – was only truly rivalled, in his pomp, by Rafael Nadal; one chalk and the other cheese. Maybe the pairings of Federer-Djokovic and Nadal-Djokovic have contained some of the best tennis ever seen, and even been next level at times, but there was always something about Nadal v Federer encounters. Roger and Rafa – the two most loved male players ever (Djokovic doesn't get a look in, in that regard, much to his sometimes obvious disdain) – seemed synonymous with good and bad, depending on your stance (though everyone knew *really* that they were both brilliant, the rivalry made in heaven), and hearts were entirely poured into their meetings. Everyone was aware that history was once more being created, as each episode unravelled before mesmerised tennis fans' eyes.

When it comes down to details, this is a rivalry that Nadal comfortably leads (23-14). You can analyse the surface and the deeper factors that have led to that. Everything means something, but on the day, Nadal had Federer's number much of the time, especially in the pair's earlier encounters. Nadal, for a time, was kryptonite to Federer. If they played now, who even knows what would happen. Last year, Roger ruled supreme. This year, Rafa, injuries aside, has looked the stronger and more consistent. His year was plagued by injuries and niggles, and bar the clay court season, he never really got going, withdrawing before (or during) most hard-court events of the season.

Speaking of injuries, Rafael, whilst five years Roger's junior – let's not forget that Mr. Nadal was considerably the younger of the two when he started winning Grand Slams (and the most likely eventuality is that Federer will have been substantially older when winning the final of his major titles) – has been blighted with injuries that have seen his absence from a number of Grand Slam tournaments. At 17, and only three behind Roger, with the age difference and the handicap of constant injuries, numbers don't tell a whole story.

Roger's game is more graceful. Than anyone's. Ever. And he has an air of superiority that both he created and has had verbally heaped upon him. He isn't humble like 'rabbit-in-the-headlights' Rafa. As soon as matches are over, the Spaniard is quiet and unassuming, while his Swiss counterpart and on-court nemesis clearly basks in the glorious spotlight – craving the adoration, the adulation – as it catches him from every angle.

Zverev Conquers and Suffers at Hands of Ruthless Federer Fans

Sascha Zverev may have ended up with tears in eyes, a cracked voice disclosing his age, and a stream of apologies – after beating Roger Federer in the semi-finals of the ATP Finals at the O2 in London – but that was always more likely than an apology from the fans of their professed tennis god Federer. It's hard not to think that Federer has fed the machine a little too much over the years, not only with his tennis, and that it's created many an atmosphere not conducive to the sport.

Today saw one of 21-year-old Zverev's finest big occasion performances ever. That, and that alone, should have been acknowledged and credited in the aftermath. That his victory – truly a fine one – was met with a huge wave of boos, that needed to be attended to by Annabel Croft's post-match interview, goes to show how far fanaticism has gone. Too far. People in the crowd were praying for their messiah to find a way to keep the match alive. It highlights that these folks cannot be fans of the sport, they are extreme fans of a man who has created much beauty on a tennis court, but is only a man, just another tennis player, albeit an exceptionally talented one. Support for Roger Federer has become like a religion. With the followers prepared to do whatever necessary to elevate Federer, without question, at the cost of every other player.

Something similar already happened once this year, at the US Open ladies' singles final. Many jumping on the 'defend Serena' bandwagon – even though any rational human being knows she behaved badly. This behaviour, of players and fans, is hugely harmful to the game and to society. It echoes existing problems, and further discussion only seems to exacerbate the issue – as poles are pulled ever further apart.

Zverev should take a bow, and wrap himself in the applause. He often seems arrogant and has an overly-expectant air regarding major success. But, today, he showed his humanity, his humility, his respect for Roger and the game, and last but clearly not least, his ability, for he played a wonderful match, a performance that ranks with his finest ever. One to put him well and truly on the map, for look who he beat. Roger may not have had a brilliant week, but he often still finds a way through (as of late) and past players. Sascha had to beat the man, his aura, and the violently biased crowd. He took it on the chin, stuck to his task, and showed a character that overcame the distractions. There are signs of definite growth early in these early days of being coached by legendary ex-player and coach Ivan Lendl. And despite the tiredness he has alluded to over this last week in his press conferences at the O2, he seemed fresh and on track; a clear plan of action executed with some pomp. His rise would be further consolidated when, a day later, he would surprise almost everyone and beat Novak Djokovic in straight sets to win his first ATP Finals title. Without the crowd to compete with on that occasion, perhaps that was easier than anyone could possibly have known.

The Zverev interview after the semi-final with Federer showed a sweetness and vulnerability that is clearly a quality in players – and in sportspeople – off the court. It certainly seemed genuine. From young German Zverev, there is an abundance of good things to come.

This Is the End...

In a flash, the 2018 tennis season has ended, the curtain has fallen (behind which there will now be holidays and pre-season training that will inevitably end up on social media), and those wonderful sporting figures have mostly long disappeared off on holiday, many to the Maldives and other exotic places. Yes, they post photos from their locations and, yes, there's an endless number of clear turquoise blue waters that their bodies are besides, inside, in front of, and so on. Their annual workload merits such a break. The need to post social media updates of their exploits is odd. Lives lived out in public. The break might even confuse the players.

The year passed in a flash. Perhaps the only way we know we get older is through our familiarity with cycles and routines; the way the world and its identical moments pass with increasing speed. Was it really almost a year since the Australian epoch of the season?

Eight Out of Eight | December 2018

Let us take stock of things at the end of 2018. The last eight women's Grand Slam winners have all been different. We have witnessed some incredible scenes in the ladies' tour in recent times, and the current depth of the game has brought a real sense of excitement to the modern age of women's tennis. There is a vibrant and eclectic mix of players in the WTA rankings who are able, on their day, to march towards a title and stand on the podium at the end, collecting silverware. We have seen scenes that will stand the test of time, with the names of worthy champions etched into some of the most beautiful trophies on earth,

The trend that 2017 started, catalysed by the absence of Serena Williams after she had won that year's first major, the Australian Open, proved itself more than a flash in the pan. Added to 2017's other Slam winners of Jelena Ostapenko (Roland Garros), Garbiñe Muguruza (Wimbledon) and Sloane Stephens (US Open), the following year finally saw Caroline Wozniacki and Simona Halep claim their maiden majors – in Australia and France respectively, as well as Angelique Kerber adding to her two majors from 2016, when she won Wimbledon. Finally, for now, another of the young breed, Naomi Osaka, broke through and saw her name etched into history, even if everyone will remember Serena's part in that final more than the victor's. Osaka won the final Slam of the year in New York's Flushing Meadows.

What does this tell us? That the WTA, at present, is rich beyond our wildest hopes and expectations. That there is plenty more to come, as the old mix in with the young (and all in-between), but unlike the men, the women can topple the living legends still playing the game. It's an exciting time, make no mistake. Then there is Daria Kasatkina and Aryna Sabalenka and more to come, and soon!

The David Goffin Pre-Season Training Video

Yesterday, David Goffin posted a video celebrating his onerous pre-season training camp. It is enlightening viewing, as we see some of the tasks he undertakes to find a high level for the start of the 2019 season, which, let's face it, will be upon us post haste.

With the literal sea of photos from beautiful spots the globe over – though mostly the Maldives – the switch from holiday mode has been made to the training of players before the new season starts in late December.

In this two-minute video, David is seen climbing cliff faces, scaling great heights, attached to a couple of short elasticated ropes as he paws his way up and down the gym room floor, lifting weights, running on a treadmill, and doing many other gym workouts. Aside from the arduous tasks he is clearly working on in the off-season, he is seen at the end of the video drinking water and eating something, proving, in no uncertain terms, that at the very least, this compact and brilliant Belgian tennis player is a living and breathing human being. The 'behind-the-scenes' look into the training and off-court exercise regime of professional players is a much more worthy snapshot of what our heroes are up to when not in the limelight, than the endless holiday photos of late.

THE
NEW
YEAR
BEGINS

A First Sighting of Veronika Kudermetova

The young 133-ranked Russian, Veronika Kudermetova, has some fearless strokes, and clubbing winners from the baseline and the net. In a first sighting of the young talent, she plays compatriot and WTA stalwart Vera Zvonareva in the quarter-finals of the Shenzhen Open in week one of 2019's competition.

Kudermetova's WTA/ATP app profile bio is yet to be filled in. She's one of the slenderer figures on tour, lending to the perennial question in such circumstances of, 'how do these players generate such ferocious power?' It isn't all about muscles, but being toned and having timing – effortless as it is to some. It's also a consideration of the men's game, as some players across both tours can generate power that others can only dream of.

Kudermetova isn't very verbal. Head down (in a work sense, not mood), confident, playing her brand of tennis that is certainly easy on the eye. It is, in fact, rather impressive.

After seeing the physio early in the third set, she seems to grow despondent (now the mood takes a tumble) when things don't go her way thereafter. Her opponent, Zvonareva, also just outside 100 at world number 109, breaks serve and then pushes towards the finishing line.

When Kudermetova finds herself 0-40 down on her next service game, at 5-3 down in the decider, it looks like she's thrown in the towel. But, she claws her way back to deuce, advantage to her, deuce again, before facing another match point. Saved. Deuce. Double fault. Another gift to Zvonareva. Big serve. Deuce once more. The back and forth continues a little longer and looks like a deadlock. Those are born to be broken. Kudermetova finally loses her patience and mildly screams something of frustration in her native Russian. The subsequent match point to Zvonareva – and sixth of the game – is then saved. The display not to go down without a fight by the youngster is a great representation of one of her chief strengths. An eighth deuce. On the seventh match point for the seasoned pro, Zvonareva clinches it, and ultimately prevails over her challenging opponent. The fighting spirit of that last game is a brilliant signal for the future of this match's losing participant. With any luck, we will be seeing much more from the young lady very soon. Watch out – both women could be inside the top 100 very soon.

Andreescu Calls for Attention Too

From that brilliant Kudermetova fight in which I eyed a new player, to another close match reaching its first set conclusion at 6-5 and another new face. This time, the even younger 18-year-old Canadian qualifier, Bianca Andreescu, in the quarter-finals over in the ASB Classic in Auckland, New Zealand.

She is taking on one of the elder stateswomen of the WTA, Venus Williams. Venus, still punching after all these years, is anything but an easy target on her day, at 38. Any signs of weakness, and she will pounce on them.

The first set ends on a tie-break as Andreescu holds serve for 6-6.

Andreescu has come through qualifying and was 152 in the world at the start of the event. That ranking will inevitably improve. As will her confidence, regardless of today's result. She doesn't give her best showing in the tie-break, muscled out by a savvier Williams (just as Kudermetova was only moments before over, in Shenzhen, by Vera Zvonareva), who takes it 7-1.

From watching Andreescu play, you wouldn't necessarily know she's only 18. From listening to her talk to her coach at the changeover after losing the first set, it becomes more apparent, though. The questioning. Of one's game. Of the young self. The game plan. All of it. So much swimming through the brain. Endless thoughts. How to turn it around? Or is it seen as gone already, given the stature of the opponent today? Her coach at the event, Virginie Tremblay of Tennis Canada, is right though, she is in the match and she can still win it. It is genuinely on her racket.

Either way, it's a fascinating composition of a match. The second set will reveal more about this extremely talented youngster. Not only are the players in the WTA rankings' upper echelons worth mentioning, others are on their way up too. Solely based on today's action, there is an enormous well of brilliance outside the top 100, scrambling and scrapping and charging as best they can to break into unknown and special terrain in the tennis world.

That weakness Andreescu showed when talking to her coach – or perhaps it is simply her age – then comes to the fore as she is broken easily by Williams at the start of the second set.

Then something special happens.

Utter domination by the qualifier. It's as if she decided just to have fun and release the cloak of expectation she had drawn around her own body. She wins six games in a row to take the second set. She had put game one behind her, found her groove, and pushed on. She breaks at the start of the third set, continuing her run of games – now four breaks of Venus' serve in a row – and serves for a 2-0 lead. This feels like watching a player become big time, whilst watching a legend of the game slipping from view. Venus failed to win her next service game as well, and before we know it the score is at 6-7 (1), 6-1, 5-0 with Andreescu only a game from another stunning victory. Then another turnaround. Venus wins three games on the trot, and another swing creates a compelling look to a final set that had appeared all but over.

Andreescu then closes the final set out 6-3. Though the outcome is irrelevant really – were it not for the manner in which it happened – it's the appearance of a new face with bags of talent that matters. It's her sixth match this week, having come through the qualifying event. It's a highly successful beginning to the year, and hopefully a platform on which the young Canadian can add further building blocks soon. Keep your eyes peeled, this woman could have something very special to offer the sport of tennis and its many worldwide spectators.

The Most Human of Modern Knights

Sir Andy Murray should take a bow. As he indicates the end of his career is seemingly nigh, and that the imminent Australian Open will be his final Grand Slam before he has his hip operated on (from which nobody knows if he will ever return), the moment is perfect to ponder his brilliance. You could ask him to take a bow for a great number of reasons from over his career – from his unrelenting ability to grow and evolve; to establishing himself at the top of the tennis tree alongside the greats Federer, Nadal and Djokovic; conquering at numerous Grand Slams and the Olympic Games on two occasions; reaching the world number one spot; his wickedly clinical support of the women's game and general social equality; his heart and willingness to show his true self, perhaps like no other player these days.

There are many more reasons.

Watching him grow from a gangly 18-year-old – under the spotlights of the world of tennis, first seen widely at Wimbledon in 2005 – he is one of the modern sporting icons who could, and should, perhaps be the most proud. The ultimate image of what a sportsperson could aspire to be, in all aspects, nowadays. He has evolved in a way that has maintained his essence, staying true to what he is and desires as a character, finding a groove with his wit and his fame, and ultimately a game that has had everything – loaded as he has been with intelligence, and every shot in the book.

THE
AUSTRALIAN
OPEN
EXTRAVAGANZA

Andy Murray: Every Ending is a New Beginning

The king of (on-court) self-deprecation, Andy Murray, has been undone at the Melbourne Arena by the in-form Roberto Bautista Agut. At the change of ends, Murray began swearing and looking like a riled man as he rued his chance to stay in the first set, on serve, as things had proceeded until 4-4.

After being broken, not only is it an impossible struggle, but it looks like Murray is being tortured, both physically and mentally. He is soon staring down the barrel of a gun, two sets to love down. That he, in typical Murray fashion, claws his way back, winning the next two sets on tie-breaks, to level the match at two sets apiece, is something only Murray could have done on this day. But, as the pair entered the last set, Bautista Agut simply had too much for the ailing Murray.

Was this his Grand Slam swansong? Is it really over here, as he had alluded to prior to the commencement of the year's first major?

The compassion in people really emerges, a true force presenting itself. For once, you can measure how well people understand a situation and appreciate its chief protagonists.

Undoubtedly, Andy Murray will go on to greatness in other areas — of tennis, and of life outside of it — and the end of his playing career will eventually mean a renewed focus with his passion, strength, and intelligence being applied to new scenarios. That may take a little time, but he has demonstrated enough over his three decades plus change, on earth so far, for those who know or observe him to question no part of his future potential.

Everything about this loss, this performance, was gutsy. The crowd was treated to a masterpiece in not giving up. If you're going to go out, *that* is how to do it. A real show of character. The final one? That remains to be seen.

The Final Set Tie-break Confusion

The newly implemented final set 'super' tie-break – that is only a fixture of the final set at the Australian Open Grand Slam – appears to fluster and confuse some of the players. Katie Boulter, in the first final set tie-break to ten ever, started to celebrate the win at 7-4 in the deciding breaker only to be told she needed three more points. The frustration at reaching the standard tie-break target, and having not yet won, is clear. Players deem the conclusion to have been reached upon marking 'seven' on the tie-break tally chart, but then need to play on and somehow find another three points. It's certainly a source of annoyance to some players as yet another set of rules applies on one of the biggest stages. With each Grand Slam taking a different tack, the issue seems somewhat hazy. Is it any wonder; even the players have no idea what is expected.

A Dip in Form / The Night Owl Effect of Naomi and Novak

There has been a dip in form. Specifically, the noticeable nosedive in Daria Kasatkina's form. Reflecting the downturn in on-court fortunes, there are many ways to start a new season. Some of the names that, for one reason or another, had a 2018 to remember haven't seen good early days in 2019. Jelena Ostapenko is winless (her last win in late September last year), Jack Sock's losing streak continues, and Kyle Edmund exited early – unlike last year, where he made a deep run at the year's first major. Andrey Rublev, Carolina Garcia, Johanna Konta, and Daria Gavrilova are ones to watch, having slipped in more recent times.

Kasatkina's breakthrough season that took her into the top 10 late last year seems a thing of the distant past as she lost her third match in a row of the young year. With all due respect, those losses were to players inferior to the Russian. She has a full spectrum of shots – a beautiful range to behold – that most players could only wish to have in their arsenals.

The most recent Grand Slam winners became night owls and made progress into the next round. Novak Djokovic won a first-round match with American qualifier Mitchell Krueger. The irrepressible Serbian was full of brilliant, stage-sweeping tennis, nigglesome shenanigans when every point and its intricacies didn't go his way (as usual), and his oft-witnessed elasticity.

Naomi Osaka, the ever-bigger draw that she is becoming post-US Open victory, is certainly one to keep the eyes peeled for. This is her first Slam since she conquered Serena in *that* match. Osaka isn't just the modern prospect we have all hoped for in the ladies' game (not that there isn't an abundance of talent on the WTA tour at present), but she's a colourful and enigmatic character. She wears her heart on her sleeve off the court as well as on, she exudes an innocence, she embraces her desire to evolve and become the type of person that has generally seen more years. She knows she isn't wise, she details her desire to get there, and she openly grows up in the public spotlight. Osaka is a modern figure with a twinkling in her eyes and a passion about life and her work – smacking fuzzy little yellow balls that opponents can seldom retrieve.

Day 5 Headlines

The Australian Open news headlines of the day (some include subheadings):

Anisimova Derails Sabalenka Bid

- 11th seed sent crashing out by youngling

Federer and Tsitsipas Set last 16 Meeting

- The old guard and the bright new hope will do battle on Sunday

Barty Surges on Home Soil

Wozniacki and Sharapova Lock Horns, The Defending Champion Ousted

Inspired Tiafoe Grabs Last 16 Berth After Five-Setter with Seppi

Fresh Berdych prevails Over Schwartzman in Four

Kvitová Sinks Bencic in Two

Bautista Agut Sees Off Khachanov Challenge in Three

Stephens and Pavlyuchenkova Set Clash

Nadal teaches Home Favourite De Minaur a Lesson

Kerber Schools Aussie Wild Card Birrell

Čilić Comeback Shows Verdasco The Exit

- Verdasco his own worst enemy as he surrenders a two-set lead and loses to Čilić in thriller

Osaka's Entrance

Despite all her own inadequacies – that she herself will point out – Naomi Osaka is a likeable young woman that crowds love. They warm to her because she is open, honest, and fun. Watching her quarter-final opponent today, Elina Svitolina, before they come on court for the match is an eye-opener. They both have headphones on, music of choice pumping into their bodies, and are in their zones; but Osaka is far calmer, and is talking to someone just out of shot, one of her team, no doubt. She is seen dancing/warming up gently, and when the camera fixes on her, she stares right at it and smiles a long, rich smile straight into the lens and down its throat.

Svitolina also offers a smile to one of the figures of authority, but she seems less relaxed than her younger opponent. Osaka, having already done it on the big stage at last year's US Open, has a sweetness and calm for her years that sets her apart from many. She hasn't been overwhelmed by her success, and looks set to rip apart the women on the other side of the net for the foreseeable future. Potentially.

Her entrance to the arena feels warming. The crowd erupts. She is hugely popular. And that is only going to grow. Her name having ever more attached to it.

Osaka exudes a peace that belies her tender age. She talks of what she needs to do to improve, to be what she wants to be, but she is already an accomplished, focused, talented, and special young lady. She's the kind of no-nonsense player that gets her head down, enjoys herself, and lets her tennis talk. Her tennis can communicate her emotions better than words.

In the other women's semi-final news, Karolina Plíšková became the final name to join Kvitová, Collins, and Osaka in the last four, beating Serena Williams as she did in three sets, and what an odd ending that was...

Something *utterly astonishing* happened in this match. At 5-1 up in the final set, Serena serves for a spot in the semis. She gets broken, then Plíšková holds serve, Serena almost breaking for victory. Another unexpected break and another hold later for Plíšková and the scoreboard is entirely different, standing at 5-5; the unthinkable a little closer. What has happened nobody is sure, but it's not something that is generally associated with Serena Williams at 5-1 up in a final set. From there, it only gets more unfamiliar. Serena loses her serve yet again, this time to love, and Plíšková holds her own nerve to successfully serve out to thirty for the match. She's bagged a hugely unlikely semi-final spot.

Petra is Boss

Petra Kvitová beats Danielle Collins in two in the last four. Two contrasting sets. The first close – a hot swamp-like heat engulfing the Czech to near-drowning point. Then, the roof was closed, a dose of good fortune administered. The action, with the roof closed, isn't even a contest as Petra comes to life, bosses proceedings, and puts her opponent in her place, her salvation complete. It ends 7-6, 6-0.

Naomi Osaka v Karolína Plíšková. In a close match, the Japanese starlet just edges out the Czech, cancelling any chance of an all-Czech ladies' final. Osaka is continuing her brilliant recent Grand Slam form. Plíšková had fought back in set two to take the match to a decider only to be pipped to the post by the reigning US Open champion, Osaka, high in confidence, 6-2, 4-6, 6-4. Once again, on the big occasion, Plíšková is found wanting. Her serve not as potent as she would have liked and Osaka hitting winners freely from all over the court; despite the Plíšková fightback the outcome was somewhat predictable. Osaka would go on to narrowly beat Kvitová – 7-6, 5-7, 6-4 – in the ladies' final to make it two majors in a row (and her first two Grand Slams) a couple of days later.

Tsitsipas plays Nadal in the second men's semi-final. Otherwise known as 'The Destruction of a Player (live)', Nadal selfishly gives his young Greek counterpart nothing, and leaves Tsitsipas wondering how on earth you can beat Federer and then be subjected to that. Tough lessons are there to be learnt from. Nadal delivering a wonderful 6-2, 6-4, 6-0 defeat to Tsitsipas.

Demolition Jobs

World numbers one and two, Novak Djokovic and Rafael Nadal, will meet in the final. They beat their semi-final opponents to the point of humiliation. You'd better believe those results hurt; wrecking-ball damage done. Defeats that state just how far ahead of the rest of the field they are right now. Playing for history as both men are – as Federer has been, too – the final will mark a huge chance to get closer to Nadal for Djokovic, or to pull four Slams clear of the Serb for the Spaniard.

On the receiving end of the punishments handed out were Stefanos Tsitsipas (by Nadal) and Lucas Pouille (By Djokovic). Nadal the wrecking-ball and Djokovic the tornado.

The final was somewhat anti-climactic. Novak Djokovic would go on to cement his return to the pinnacle of men's tennis by winning a third consecutive Slam by beating Nadal easily, 6-3, 6-2, 6-3. A comprehensive Grand Slam triumph. Nobody could have stopped him. Nadal had been by far and away the second-best man in the men's draw, and this wasn't even close.

Point Construction

Some players simply pummel a range of winners and are left wanting when facing superior opponents. They fall short against stronger opponents – those who are savvier and more skilful; the ones who can endure the greater, and so on.

Stronger players have physical attributes and tactical know-how, mental understanding and fortitude, the ability to execute a plan, or (if needed) revert to a plan B, C, or an entire alphabet of alternatives. They can find never-ending solutions to the problems posed on court. See Simona Halep, Andy Murray, and now Naomi Osaka for examples of this on a regular basis.

In Melbourne, the way that Novak Djokovic manoeuvred his opponents around the court knowing what was coming, and knowing they would eventually submit, was inspiring. His game management meant he would head off into the sunset with the point, the set, and the match. If you construct points – effortlessly, intelligently, with an understanding of the geometry of the court (and consistently hit those extreme targets) – well, you are going to be hard to topple from your rather elevated post. As the Serb undeniably is.

Federer: Ton Up

One of Roger Federer's remaining tasks in the game seems to be to chalk up as many records as possible, before he makes his way out the 'exit' door. He clearly has a new strategy, compared to previous years, and is playing events that will boost his ranking this year and take him back to the crowds he has missed out in the last few seasons or so. He was never going to bow out before reaching the lofty scales of his hundredth title, which he won at the Dubai Championships today. He was never going to vanish with a low ranking and early losses in many tournaments. This is Roger Federer after all. Whether you love him, or not, he has changed tennis and done so for the better.

While he might now struggle to catch the only player with more titles (mind you, don't bet against this!) – Jimmy Connors on 109 – he has shown himself far ahead of his own generation, predominantly based on how late in his thirties he has been able to keep going at such a high level for. Will Nadal and Djokovic, who are half a decade younger, be able to follow suit? I think nature and even the staunchest fans of those players might doubt it.

So, another score settled, indeed, as he brings up 100 on his title tally chart. And some. Masters events in Indian Wells and Miami are fast rolling around, meaning Federer has his eye in, and is ready for a fresh assault at those key early Masters titles of 2019. Federer has had a nice little warm up in Dubai, ticked another of his remaining 'tennis bucket list' items off, and will feel good. Which makes him dangerous. Very much so. Tsitsipas, who has been put in his place after knocking Federer out of his Australian Open title defence back in January, will feel it isn't guaranteed that he can beat the top guys yet. While the young Greek has himself sneaked into the top 10 for the first time (ranked ten on 4th March 2019), Federer has reasserted himself as one to beat over three sets. Of course, he was never going to rescind to the younglings on a regular basis, not even now, and certainly not without a graceful fight.

In February last year, Federer became the oldest world number one ever. A little over a year on, and another big record is logged, as he reaches his hundredth title and separates himself even further from the crowd. The January changing of the guard naturally mentioned at the time of Tsitsipas's Melbourne defeat of Roger was, as expected, softly brushed aside, both in the first meeting on court since and psychologically by Federer, ever the man to learn and frustrate his opponents anew. Tsitsipas has much to learn and such defeats will show him he isn't yet where he perhaps believed he was. He isn't far off though, let's face it.

Confidence – Finding a Rich Vein of Form

Playing oneself into form, by overcoming external factors and influences isn't easy. Perhaps the shutter that allows those outside forces inside, to tamper with a player's natural ball striking and tactical ability, needs to be closed. Draw those curtains and shut the world out, focus on yourself alone, and your game. Allow your tennis to breathe, like a living being; permit it to grow and reach for greatness.

Confidence is a strange thing. You need to win to get it, it doesn't just appear. So, how do you get the wins to build it, when what you are lacking is the very source of all that is good, and which propels you toward magnificence. Well, the shutter is of great value to enable your natural ability to emerge, to do what it is capable of.

Seeing players as hollow husks – just shells of what they were before, flailing and missing the targets they previously hit for fun – is hard. Seeing Kasatkina now, and Ostapenko for some time, as well as Jack Sock and others simply unable to reach their previous heights, is quite unfortunate. Everyone cannot be expected to sustain best form permanently, but again, this is testament to just how good those who live at the top truly are. Getting there is one thing; retaining those positions requires some serious attitude and consistent hard work.

Therefore, I have been responsible for the willing on of Jelena Ostapenko and Daria Kasatkina. It's a wonderful thing to see young people becoming attuned to the wider world, finding themselves, and making a mark – surging like electricity to near the top of the game (sometimes even the very pinnacle; see, for example, Naomi Osaka), water fit to burst a dam. When that ascent is followed by a descent that is hard to deal with, it requires the mathematical equations of tennis to be brought in and analysed.

Later in the year, Ostapenko would be a little unlucky to get Kiki Bertens, last year's runner up, in round two of the Madrid Open. Nevertheless, and despite really enjoying Bertens and feeling she warrants a little more attention and respect, you can't help but find yourself cheering Ostapenko on, knowing what we do about her ability, and her rich, sweet character. The same is true for Daria Kasatkina, who has also had a dramatic downturn in her results since the end of last year. She was moving nicely up the ranking ladder only to find a loss of form that is still lasting, derailing her ascent and sending her in completely the wrong direction. Both young players showing all the potential in the world means nothing if you lose confidence and/or do not have the right team around you.

The Kyrgios Switch Is Off Again

Nick Kyrgios the enigma. Nick Kyrgios the lackadaisical tennis artist and talent. His recent Acapulco title, beating three top-tenners en-route – Rafael Nadal, John Isner and Sascha Zverev – and overcoming Nadal's multiple match points (and playing some mind-blowing tennis) else proved his talent. However, consistency fails to attend to a player invaded more by mental difficulties than anything. It's clear – he has the game, in spades. He is one of the uniquely special players of the age, with a natural laid-back style that (when firing) can put anyone to the sword.

Therefore, bringing such form into Indian Wells, being drawn to face none other than top seed Novak Djokovic in round three, and an all-round feeling of an upturn in Kyrgios' on court fortunes, meant the days ahead were exciting. Once again, consistency has deserted Kyrgios. He loses to an inferior player in Philipp Kohlschreiber and therein abandons the chance to back up his recent success – winning the Acapulco title with some big attention-grabbing wins - and throw the cat amongst the Indian Wells pigeons (they are everywhere; they have them in the desert still, right?). How many chances to advance will Kyrgios allow to escape, like rogue spanners finding their way into the works? Yet again. One step forward, two steps back. One of the key attributes of a top tennis players is consistency. Look, even now, at the form of Nadal, Federer, and Djokovic, over lengthy periods of months and years. That ability to produce one's best is what elevates them to the top of the game. Many players have fine results throughout the year. Very few replicate them on a regular basis. And there we have a simple statement that defines the important struggle and the targeted desire for (possibly) all professionals of the game.

Kyrgios can switch it on and off like the rest of us do lights, and it's curious to ponder quite why he is determined to pull against everything that sets him apart, smothering the flame of what makes him so special. It's the easy way out not to be bothered. Work hard, persevere, and flick that switch on. The results would be spectacular.

The Hsieh Acknowledgement

One thing is certain, no player will like to see Hsieh Su-wei's name even remotely close to their own in any tournament draw. She is a lethal floater, immune to big names and fearless in the face of the dangers that others cower from. That attitude has lit the torch paper, seeing some of her biggest ever results over the past couple of seasons.

With the Chinese Taipei player's mix of stamina, slice, and power, and her never-ending spirit to seek solutions on court and frustrate opponents, she's the ultimate on-court challenge when at her best. In fact, when in her groove, she looks practically unbeatable. It never quite brings her the big titles, though she gets a sniff at least. All of that, not to mention the fun and joy she brings to the court, is further balanced and highlighted by her smile, her sense of humour and her charm. While her English isn't anywhere near perfect, she lights up stadia with her post-match interviews and bouncy, joyous jokes and mischievous nature. She is needed and brings something that few players do. Truly, she seems to appreciate what she does, and the privileged position she finds herself in. How could anyone begrudge this skinny titan her stunning results as she has conquered players from Halep and Muguruza to Plíšková and Kerber.

Her on-court coaching sessions reveal her body language, her ability to listen, look the other way, take everything on board, and then go away and immediately implement the advice. Sometimes, she misses a fist-bump, and doesn't always pair up communicatively, yet she is enigmatic, and a smile is never far from her lips. While she sometimes looks bored while receiving said advice, she shows great respect for her coach.

She's a wonderful role model, a past doubles world number one and multiple Grand Slam doubles title winner. She's a perennial puzzle for the other women to solve (very few come close), and she warrants a measured acknowledgement of her unique on-court prowess. Hsieh Su-wei, I doff my cap to thee.

WTA Newsflash

It is Indian Wells. Bianca Andreescu is still in, Naomi Osaka is out. Barring possibly Petra Kvitová and Osaka herself, I cannot help but feel the best player in the world right now is teenage sensation Bianca Andreescu. She's the 18-year old Canadian who appears to own 2019, who received a memo that nobody else did, who is tearing up the rulebook and storming the world of women's tennis a la Monica Seles/Martina Hingis. Something about this fresh star's physical prowess reminds me of Nadal, Serena, (enter your own player here). She has huge weapons that are working well, in full swing; a flow that, once turned on, is hard to stop, limit, or placate in any way whatsoever.

Kerber v Andreescu
(Indian Wells Ladies' Final 2019)

Bianca Andreescu, the surprise package of the year thus far, will have gone from outside the world's top 150 players to inside the top 50. If she wins Indian Wells, she'll be ranked around 25; if she loses around ten spots lower.

Angelique Kerber needs little introduction, and in a tournament in which many of the fancied names have fallen by the wayside, leaving an oddly attractive final weighted in favour of the older and more experienced player, she will feel this is a golden opportunity. However, there is also some uncertainty given Andreescu's run, and her splendid form of the year so far. Also, the young Canadian has nothing whatsoever to lose, and she has been playing that way.

Andreescu is dangerous. She is composed, unfamiliar with such a platform for her tennis voice, a stage of this size, and she has confidence (nay, almost arrogance), and freedom of youth on her side. You can see it in her play, how she walks onto the court, and her interviews – composed, full of belief as well as a good measure of fun and enjoyment. But, her play is remarkable. The way she approaches it all, attacking balls and sending them all over the court, painting lines, filling the corners up with post-fuzzy yellow ball arrow markings. The way she patiently outlasts her opponent on the longer points, revelling in pouncing on anything and everything, showcasing her undeniable talent. She'll be around fifth in the race to Singapore after less than three full months of the calendar year, a season already full of surprises. From nowhere. Imagine if everyone starting the year around 150 had such a surge into the upper echelons of the game. The rankings would be chaos. It is almost unheard of, though, and that is why it is so very special. This is a real mark she is making, a breakthrough year, and a talent to regard with close attention over the years to come. This woman looks like a champion in the making.

How do you get to be this tough, this rock solid and undaunted on the big stage, at this tender age? How do you become impervious to all the forces, conditions, and factors involved in such elite level sport? She's going to win this match, with weapons that are frustrating Kerber, even driving her crazy. Right now, she looks like the best player in the world, young Andreescu does. A huge shock on the cards, looming, as she takes charge of the final. She takes the first set.

She is then nudged off her pedestal in the second set, and Kerber takes it to a concluding set. It's an entertaining and thrilling final.

Extraordinary scenes. Anything you can do I can do better, as Andreescu double breaks Kerber (at first breaking back after Kerber had gained the initial upper-hand of the final set, only to lose the advantage) to lead 5-3, and is able to smell victory. She serves for the title. Fails. Then has a crack at Kerber's serve, does enough and breaks to win. A big one.

Her *first* big one.

Wow.

The WTA Tour is in Exceedingly Good Shape

The state of the WTA at present is impressive; frightening, in fact. When the ladies line up for the larger events, any of a substantial portion of those faces could end up with the trophy beside them. Predictions, bets, and form almost go out the window; indeed, for punters, only wild shots in the dark pay off in the end. Quite how on earth to predict the eight women at the year-end event in Shenzhen – that gathers the best eight players of the calendar year – for 2019, one can only wonder.

At a time in which the men's tour still, somehow, remains relatively predictable (is that about to change?) and has the same three men picking up the Grand Slam titles, the women's tour has a near endless factory-line of different products, each offering something dynamic and of great interest, to both the close tennis observer and those who dip in and out.

Yesterday's WTA title win for wild card (the first time ever here in California) Bianca Andreescu again signals the up-and-comers, and their ability to shift expectation and shock the world. The 18-year-old began 2019 outside of the world's top 150. She is now ranked 24 with Ostapenko (23) and Kasatkina (22) immediately above her. Who would've said – based on their past exploits – that such a scenario would happen? As those two young players struggle to find form – even their own tennis selves – a much younger woman has appeared from practically nowhere to head, almost unassumingly, for the top of the game.

Strength in depth in the women's game is again shown by Hsieh Su-wei and her sometime surges at big events, usurping and nudging top players from their pedestals. She has become a nemesis on big day matches to many a top tenner in recent years, somehow getting better as she gets older; wilier and in control of her sublime range of tennis skills and shots.

The David Ferrer Time Machine

When the Spanish stalwart, David Ferrer, saw the Miami Open draw and his potential second-round meeting with Sascha Zverev, I'd love to know what went through his head. "Why not?" perhaps. Maybe, like his countryman Nadal, he says he never looks that far ahead, focusing only on the first match, as beyond means nothing until you arrive there. Other players wouldn't want to play the gangly and talented under-achieving (would he himself have expected only three Masters titles and to be the ATP Finals champion of 2018 by now?) German. He is becoming increasingly unpredictable on the big stage, something a little odd given his coach of some time now, Ivan Lendl. Frustration felt by all parties, no doubt.

From watching Zverev's mannerisms and expressions on court, you can't help but feel he is his own worst enemy, that he has got it all wrong upstairs, in the mental department. Nobody could deny his on-court promise, surely. But a champion, one to join the other greats and lesser legends, needs to have *all* the attributes to force Grand Slam victory. This is a step many would have expected of Zverev already, not to mention the man himself and his father – the other key member of his coaching team. Are events off-court proving distracting? Such weaknesses are something the wonderful Spanish leech, Ferrer, feasts upon.

The pressure Zverev has applied on himself (greater than maybe any other player at present) is a burden that sees the player take steps forwards (see the aforementioned 2018 ATP Finals) but then backtrack with petulant behaviour that earmarks him as a less lovable top player. Maybe he doesn't care about being liked, but again he isn't helping the overall impression he provides the public and tennis world with. David Ferrer comes across as the opposite – much shorter, positive, never giving up, no anger; just love, passion and fight, his own compass leading his way, his heart its autopilot. He and others who have stood on the other side of a net from Zverev, are there to show, to teach, to indicate the way to go. Not for the sake of following. Zverev simply doesn't listen, he doesn't open his senses to the lessons there; like many young people nowadays, he believes he already knows it all. It is not the case. At all.

At the start of this year, I had an idea of the Slam winners for the year ahead. Whilst not enjoying his on-court behaviour and general demeanour, I pencilled the young Zverev in as the Wimbledon men's winner for 2019. That looks a way off. If he hits a groove, it could happen, but his attitude needs shelling and shaking, leaving totally behind. It's him and Kyrgios with the most unfulfilled talent; few could deny that. While there is still time, are we seeing the likes of Tsitsipas, Shapovalov, Tiafoe, Auger-Aliassime, Medvedev, Khachanov, et al. catch and overtake the German? Well, it could well happen, could be on the cards, maybe in the stars.

No introduction to David Ferrer and his approach is needed. He's just the sort of player to keep going and turn the screw when it comes to his opponents displaying weaknesses and rendering themselves there for the taking. Zverev shouldn't be losing matches like these, no matter how well Ferrer turns back the clock.

David Ferrer stands on the other side of the net, craving further wins before he soon hangs up his racket. What his 37-year-old body might be prompting, his mind clearly does not agree with. There is more fight in a little finger of this man than most players. He is battling against age, wrestling logic, determined to go down with a smile, with a soaked brow, and with the knowledge that he gave his all.

And so, Señor Ferrer successfully turns back the clock. He adds another highlight to his impressive bank of results, and signals that the post-Madrid Open retirement date he has set will come only too soon. If only his time machine was a permanent acquisition and not a loaner. Nevertheless, these are times to remember, and Ferrer and his people have every reason to be proud. He is about to leave one remarkable legacy as a player, and there is a softly-spoken *gentleman* behind that never-say-die tennis approach. It's all about heart when it comes down to it. We don't want our players to be machines; we want them to be living and breathing forces that inspire and love and play with everything they've got. Nothing less.

Ashleigh Barty Cracks the Top Ten

Ashleigh Barty throws her name into the ring for the future majors. She completely outplays and out-thinks Karolína Plíšková in the Miami Open ladies' final. Plíšková is a player who – in the bigger moments of her career and those key matches – seems to over-think things and precipitate her own downfall. Barty doesn't need on-court coaching on this occasion. She is a woman who knows what she is about, knows what she can do, how she can hurt her opponents, where she is headed. It's refreshing to see such confidence and yet not fear a step any closer to arrogance.

Barty is one of the few players who is an utter delight to watch, no airs or graces to her game, her character, she clearly loves the sport and protects it with her performances, whilst being a passionate Aussie, and a concise and well-spoken interviewee. She serves effortlessly. She shows flair and finesse and utter focus. Nothing and nobody are coming in-between her and that Miami Open title today (and they do not, Plíšková beaten in two sets). You have to say, that if she can take that form, that attitude, that style of play into a major, she will find a crown atop her head sometime soon.

Roger Federer Has
Everlasting Batteries

If the attempted Sunshine double (Indian Wells and Miami Masters titles) and what preceded it in 2019 has proven anything – already documented time and again over recent years – it is that Roger Federer has something nobody else does, namely batteries that last infinitely. It doesn't really matter who is placed before him these days, if he is in form – forget the maturing body that shows few signs of his real age, or much by way of wear and tear – he will probably still win. Often with some aplomb.

While he leads the ATP race to London for the men, it's surely the performances that have impressed the most. He often starts an event looking beatable, a little uncertain, and mostly ends looking the clear winner. Four events so far this year. Two titles (in Dubai and Miami), one runner-up spot (to Dominic Thiem in the recent Indian Wells final), and a mid-tournament exit at the Australian Open, where he failed to defend his title, meeting his match in young Greek Tsitsipas. This stirs the thought that the three-set format suits Roger perfectly these days, a true reflection of the gulf between the Grand Slam five-set format and the one that the rest of the annual calendar witnesses. I am more than aware that, in the upcoming Slams this summer, it is more than likely he will prove me wrong. If he can keep his matches short, which has perhaps been the key for a while now, especially when adding up each round of a Grand Slam event, then he has a chance. His evolving yet faithful style sees him able to execute a game plan, even adapt, and find a way to pass players now much younger. Players who will be infuriated to be still having the great of the game submerge their hopes and dreams. He is as large and looming an opponent as ever he has been. You can make mistakes against him, but he nearly always punishes them, and if they mount up – chances are you will lose that match. Simple maths.

His batteries show no sign of slowing down. If Roger really was considering retiring at the end of this season, and only results would fuel that decision, then the first part of the 2019 season tells us he will still be here at the turn of the decade. He simply has too much to offer still. While the target of Connors' 109 titles does look a tough ask, Federer now standing tall with 101 of his own, the chance to defend the Miami title 12 months down the line (and who knows what comes next) may prove a little too tempting to refuse. Not to mention a close run at Indian Wells only two weeks earlier. This is art, this is passion, this is a hunger for more. There is a hunger only rivalled and matched by Djokovic and Nadal. Pete Sampras' once magnificent shining record of 14 Grand Slam titles has been truly obliterated by this trio.

The Youth Brigade

Finally, there comes a changing to the face of tennis, both to the men (slowly) and the women. Having grown used to seeing the same individuals, those perennial winning culprits refusing to let others on the podium, there eventually must be an end and a new beginning. Those who failed to topple the best of a generation have been and gone and, now, the ageing process and a fierce new crew of talented youngsters are responsible for a slowly-shifting tide, a new face to global tennis.

The signal in shifting seasons – turning the clocks forward one hour at the end of March –moves our attention to the clay and then grass courts of Europe. Europe hosts a veritable feast of tennis action on sun-dappled bright orange-red courts, and verdant grass lawns. This year, it means an invasion of hot young talent across both the women's and men's games of world tennis.

If you watch tennis all year round, you will have familiarised yourself with some of the faces attached to these hot young properties. For what seems like aeons, we have been talking about the next generation, the ones to usurp Roger, Rafa, and Novak, and Serena and her now-fading generation. It never quite seemed to happen, but few with an eye fixed on this year's results can deny that while Roger continues to be sublime, and while Serena continues to be an enigma, nobody could second-guess the future results of 'those kids'. Actually, 'those kids' are now 'these kids', and are flying up the rankings with a flamboyant modern swagger, a panache to deliver it all impatiently.

With few examples of these younglings securing the bigger titles, it is surely only a matter of time as they impress on the bigger stages and are often beaten by experience more than anything else. They are exploding onto a scene they plan on dominating over the next decade plus. The year, so far, has been defined by Andreescu in the ladies', and Felix Auger Aliassime – whose form has been a breath of fresh air – in the men's games. The two 18-year-olds have shot up the respective rankings from the relative oblivion of outside the top hundred. While Felix hasn't quite packed the punch of Andreescu, he has been a wonder on the men's side and there is much more to come from him. The pair are now jostling near the top, only a little behind the likes of many of their childhood idols.

MADE
FROM
CLAY

Monte Carlo Masters
Men's Final 2019

Surprise, surprise! No Nadal v Djokovic final. Neither man present in the final showcase, as the year twists and turns in unexpected ways. Dušan Lajović and Fabio Fognini face off in a wholly fresh-looking and compelling final.

At 1-1, Lajović gets a break of the Fognini serve and continues with the form of his life – surging. You cannot understate the impact of world number 48 – Serbian Lajović – being in a Masters final. The beauty of today (after recovering from the shock of the final line-up) is that whoever wins will be a Masters champion for the first time. Maybe neither man will have the chance again, for who knows what lies ahead. Never a better hope. Seize the day!

Fognini, the same guy who ripped apart the King of Clay (Nadal) a day earlier, was too strong, too on a roll, and simply too much for Lajović. After breaking back in the first set, there was only one man in charge. He conquered 6-4, 6-3. His first Masters title bagged, here, that Italian swagger and bravado oozing from his body, in his early thirties (much as Isner at Miami 2018, and the approaching-thirty Del Potro at Indian Wells 2018), displaying a belief that might have been attained as a result of the passing years.

Discovering Laslo Đere

Laslo Đere has got his mojo working. Look up the story. I'll not echo a well-documented background. To reiterate the spectacle is to reduce the man's progress on a tennis court and evolution as a man. Reduce no man to solely his story. He is not a simple cartoon caricature. While, yes, our backgrounds define us, do we want them dragged up every single time we step outside into daylight, every time we take to the court, centre stage at work?

The man deserves a spotlight thrown his way, illuminating his abilities and his future, driven by a deep-seated desire to prove himself. He has mapped a course nobody saw coming in early 2019 and is surely one of the romantic tennis stories of the year, and will remain so come its end. Everybody wants the human angle, that which they can fall in love with; some Disney fairy-tale that pulls the audience in. In this case, it's rather gruesome. The romanticism of dark spots, the glow of those events, echoes ever louder in modern life.

Having won his first ATP title at the Rio Open earlier in the year (beating Dominic Thiem in round one and slaying the scorching new kid on the block Felix Auger-Aliassime in the final*), he now looks a challenging proposition on the tennis court, making the latter rounds of multiple tournaments he shows up at. He has a ranking that is soaring – currently stationed inside the top thirty for the first time in his career – and there is plenty of time to go and room for improvement marching him into the ever higher echelons of the sport.

*It is recommended to track down a video of Đere's winner's speech – a real beauty!

Introducing... The Barcelona Open

The blue AstroTurf carpet walkway that leads up to the main courts – where the best live action is viewed – celebrates several sponsors and food stalls as it arcs from its early beginnings at the entrance. There are booths where you can have a minor hit with racket and ball – a magnet to the kids, of course. There is a Rafael Nadal Academy stand, and ones for Peugeot, for Espanyol, one of the main football teams of the city, and much more.

To go into further detail, there is a Mapfre insurance stall, and tennis paraphernalia for sale, as well as other ways to fritter away money and shower ones' kids with keepsakes from the event (even though they chiefly scout signatures from their heroes on the giant 20 euro tennis balls). Isdin, the skincare company, is on the left, Ben and Jerrys on the right, followed by a hotdog van, and a place to buy *gofres* before some more gourmet food and drink options. Then, there's a combination of shadows and the main stadium towering a little over. Entering early, you have a moment to savour this, before the remainder of the public launches itself inside, injecting the venue with life and tennis fanaticism; swamping the blue path with bodies, a sea of crisscrossing bodies.

You can feel how much the bodies – jostling and excitedly discussing a range of tennis-related topics – feed off the sport, not only coming from nearby, but from far and wide, to watch idols and fellow natives from other lands.

Unlike yesterday, the sun is beating down, and a breeze is making itself known: a beautiful Barcelona spring day. People are gently milling around, relaxed before the main singles action of the day begins. Players are practising on the other courts. Centre court awaits Daniil Medvedev and Nicolás Jarry.

The vibrant golden green of the trees complements the sky blue behind and above them. The centre court stands slowly fill up in anticipation of Medvedev's clash with Jarry. To the less informed, it should be stated that Medvedev is now a top player and to see him live – his skinny Russian frame creating some wonderful power and intrigue – is a 2019 highlight of the tour, although there exist several versions of the enigmatic fellow. He is capable of both wowing and frustrating his audience and opponent, for different reasons.

Medvedev is one of the finest young players in the world, constantly working on improving both on and off the court, taking baby steps, the kind that lead to giant strides over time. He is on an upward trajectory and has been for some time now, one of the form players of the year thus far (he lost in the Brisbane International final and won the Sofia Open in the early stages of the season).

The hustle and bustle of the tennis crowd as it finds its seats and settles is soothing. The Catalan tempo perfect for this blowy spring day; the upper stands have a cool wind whipping around the ears and neck as the two players warm up, and the doubles match on court one behind – visible from our seats in the press section – gets underway. This tennis club, in the sunshine not seen yesterday, has a real sense of history and beauty.

The sometime disconnection between players and crowd is fascinating. Depending on nationality, surface, weather, mood (of player, of crowd, of everyone else), it varies. And Medvedev pushes the wrong buttons with this crowd, as with others, very easily, almost testing their characters, as his own is tested on court.

The number of people entranced by their phones, oblivious to the tennis as it is being played, is somewhat remarkable though. It's a bond that is denying mankind its inherent opportunity to live and experience and absorb. It's difficult to follow tennis with phone glued to hand.

A sun-baked clay court really does echo its accompanying season, part beach and kids' sandpit and part elite sporting arena. The funny bounces of the ball on clay are unique and frustrating in equal measure. Clay can witness the occasional odd bounce – the ball can fade away as it hits the ground or kicks up in otherworldly fashion.

The crowd starts to tire of Medvedev and some of his reactions and irritation, its own sense of annoyance voiced and tossed all over the Russian like a blanket. When we think back to our own twenties and how feisty we were (at least a portion of us), some of the behaviour of Medvedev and Kyrgios, to name but a couple, doesn't seem so terribly impetuous.

The crowd has reacted to Medvedev's frustration and has started whistling, ready to jeer, all too easily descending into a madness to accompany that of any player reacting in a way natural to them. It's a truly enigmatic side to the sport. Cheers for Jarry increase, which increase the Russian's irritation. Tellingly, though, he keeps a lid on matters and crosses the finish line in great style. He is surely a curious and wonderful watch.

The stands are full of movement, everybody shifting, a constant desire to relocate. It's as if the stands are pumped full and then sucked dry of the self-same bodies again between games, at the change of ends, and when sets finish, but especially, and more naturally, in-between matches. The court is then revamped, prepared with a good raking and watering, with a change of ball kids and lines-people and a new umpire. All set to go again. Ready to deliver the rich entertainment of professional tennis.

The rustle, the low hum, the buzz. A smattering of applause as Kei Nishikori finds the early break of Felix Auger-Aliassime's serve. The young Canadian has a few stray shots, Nishikori turns the screw, knowing how to pounce on an opponent's weaknesses and uncertainty. An overcast sky hangs above; a grey, cool Barcelona in spring.

Auger-Aliassime holds serve in game two of set two – after being dispatched easily in set one by his older rival – and is visibly pumped. The crowd, getting behind him, is also buoyed by his refusal to back down easily to the seasoned Nishikori. Clay, a fresh proposition, seemingly poses more problems for Felix and he is accepting of the new challenge, ever ready to soak up and learn from the experience. Nishikori prevails 6-1, 6-3.

The different grunts of nationality are on display as Dominic Thiem and Jaume Munar slug it out. The noises follow the sound of balls popping off strings and almost sound like their own separate contest – a grunting race. No clear winner to that contest, although Thiem wins the tennis match 7-6, 6-1.

There is thick cloud above, and occasional raindrops that later turn into heavier rain during the Nadal-Ferrer encounter. The stands become increasingly packed. This is a fascinating introduction to the event and has just the tennis to capture the attention.

Rafael Nadal is a world. Everything else orbiting him. The television mannerisms, tics, those famed idiosyncrasies are not the same as the real-life ones. Here, the caricature is gone, loaded with the physical presence and accompanying doubt, nuance and magnificence missing on TV. Nadal, in person, on a tennis court, absolutely is a bull. An astonishing sporting sight to behold. Despite the rain coming and going, playing with us all, holding the puppet strings as it does, Nadal conquers his special and professionally outgoing compatriot, David Ferrer, 6-3, 6-3 in a fun and magical encounter.

The sun finally comes out and blows the clouds out of sight. The shadows are thrown across the clay; some of the markings are like grooves on a vinyl record, where feet, and shoes, have dragged across the surface – poetic gliding. Tsitsipas wins the second set against Struff, and levels the match. The clay slate is wiped clean, ready for a new work to be recorded.

Soon the sun drops behind the buildings in the nearby background, and the court is now entirely covered in shade, just a sliver poking through to the eyes of Tsitsipas as he is broken by Struff for the second time in the final set. Can the German hold his serve this time to make it count and take a 5-2 lead? He holds to love and has three game chances to win the match – one on his own serve. He takes the first chance to set up a meeting with the King of Clay, one Mr. Nadal, tomorrow.

Stefanos Tsitsipas didn't seem able to impose himself on his opponent today, Jan-Lennard Struff, and consequently succumbs in something of a subdued fashion in three sets, having brought himself back into the match's reckoning by winning the second set. He clearly has the game and the flair. In a season where he has many points to defend and is still developing in many senses, perhaps it is too much to expect for him to still turn up to events, in his best form, every week.

After all the magical singles of the day, we witness the start of Jamie Murray and Bruno Soares' doubles match before the unexpected clawing cold drives us to head for the hotel while the action continues.

The live tennis experience is saturated with a range of emotions you simply do not get when watching it on television. From the unfiltered live atmosphere, to the sounds of umpires and lines-people, to the ball kids scurrying. There are movements and noises and the visual splash of clay when shots land and kick up. It's a veritable picnic for those spectators fortunate enough to be in attendance.

What A Rally! / Ghost of a Racket

At 3-3, 15-15 in the final set of their Barcelona Open semi-final, Medvedev and Nishikori do a dance and share a 40-shot exchange. A rally from the heavens, to the spectator if not the players involved. What a rally! Sometimes the whole world, the soul of a match, of everything being observed, is captured in one point – a universe, a microcosm, a telling moment in time. Nishikori wins the point and Medvedev, who might then have a shoulder slump, responds to win the next three points and keep his nose marginally in front. A telling response. It has felt like one of those points that a match could hinge on, be defined by, and yet, it seems not. Medvedev swatted it away like any other annoying fly buzzing around, getting in his way. This expansion of his on-court presence is phenomenal.

It makes you think about the larger picture and how each small moment, each point – the energy rising and falling – pieces together into one giant, perfect puzzle, somehow. Matches have, of course, repeatedly hinged, twisted, and turned upon points such as just witnessed.

At the end of the second set, Medvedev's racket was smashed into the ground. Can someone sew it back together again and send it to a poor kid that would love to play tennis; that would cherish what he had in his hands? Does that racket really need to die such a tragic death, a sudden blitz of emotion pushing it violently out of the door marked 'emergency exit'? Think of all those rackets, celebrated with numerous grotesque replays on the television, documenting the ugliest sides of players in their explosive glory. Think of the graveyard of stringed weapons, of the different breaks to those frames, and the shapes, and the destruction, the pure intention to destroy. Is it not better the destruction of an opponent through one's play instead of submitting another racket to the spiritual cemetery of players' instruments? And the spirit of the racket goes where? And what of the body, deceased, beyond repair, eternally broken, a memory to some, gone to all.

The Rise and Fall of Jelena Ostapenko

The Latvian wonder-kid may not be the first to suffer such a fate but, at present, it is certainly noticeable as the French Open (the location of her stunning victory almost two years ago, and only a couple of days into her twenties), is looming. A decline in status, in results, in mood at work on-court can be temporary – especially if one has found the surroundings of an elevated position with young years – but, how do you stop the slide? How do you prevent it becoming a total descent? Consolidating ones' achievements cannot be easy, nor repeating the impossible – a task this young lady knows all about. Jelena Ostapenko is known. Her accomplishments are not small, but being dwarfed somewhat by what is now happening. However, she will *always* be a Grand Slam champion.

The focussed on-court character took her smiley and friendly demeanour into interviews and everywhere else she would go, a refreshing young face for the modern game. A sprinkling of Latvian charm, a peppering of youthful wonder, and more than a dash of enchantment from a lethal racket: the kid came good. Those characteristics are slipping, although she is still only in the last months before turning 22.

She had climbed to as high as five in the world by late 2017 (the year of her shock Roland Garros title win), and ever since her stock has plummeted and continues to do so.

While 2018 did see some good matches and endeavours, such as a run at Wimbledon (where the expectations were lower), it clearly underlined a lack of confidence that she has carried into 2019 as her ranking fall resembles a horror show. She rarely wins a match these days, and it's only so long before that leads you to Jack Sock-esque obscurity. You can't fluke what she did in Paris in 2017 (seven matches are too much for that), of course.

Being the one others wanted to topple didn't sit well with Ostapenko at her tender age (Osaka also seems to have her own uncomfortable moments), and now the fun needs to return to her game. It was the fun that made it all such a fairy-tale – the smile, the free hitting, the total abandonment when she struck those winning shots – from all over the court in Paris. 2017 seems so very long ago.

The fall of this young star (with plenty of time to rise like a phoenix from the ashes again) needs halting, and a positive team needs to rebuild the foundations of this woman again. Get things together, and she can head in the right direction of the rankings and the game once more, with renewed passion and success.

Garin and Berrettini

Cristian Garin and Matteo Berrettini are two for the clay court season of 2019, both having made waves thus far. Meeting here at the Bavarian International – in an incredibly close final – only strengthened their claims as a pair to watch over the coming weeks.

While nobody expects either of these men to win Roland Garros (though who knows), much like Cecchinato last year, a good run at the year's second Slam might not look out of the question. Both players are beating strong opposition, evenly matched as they are.

Here are a couple of men who know the importance of having a strong clay court season. For players who favour the surface, and mostly grew up hitting endless balls that picked up and kicked up the orange-brown clay, this is the time to cash in on that experience. It's a moment to gather some momentum to then harvest and take into the remainder of the season, across grass and hard courts alike. While it's not easy for many players to switch between the three surfaces, and many have a favourite surface and one for which their game is more naturally suited, confidence does play a huge part in the career of elite sportspeople.

Garin emerges the victor 6-1, 3-6, 7-6.

The Mladenovic Addition

Finally, with my plea for the Kristina Mladenovic camp to add a new (non-family) coach to the team having been observed, they – and of course she – can get moving back in the right direction in the singles rankings. A talented player with what seems like a fragile mind, Kiki should be punching at a higher weight than she has in the past year. It's seen a disastrous descent down the rankings from hitting a peak of ten in the world in 2017. In fact, 2017 saw her best singles tennis thus far – what she was truly capable of – following her doubles-split with Caroline Garcia who also went on to have her best season yet in the singles.

Mladenovic brings an old-fashioned grace and charm to the tennis court, a throwback to decades before, and most unlike other modern players. Almost trapped in the wrong era, she has shown what she can do, swinging at her finest, and plenty would like to see her return to those ways. Let us not forget, as is often shown, that she is amongst the very elite of ladies' doubles players (she will soon be crowned the ladies' doubles world number one) with an increasing tally of major triumphs with her now partner, Hungary's Tímea Babos.

Ferrer Ready to Bow Out

A Masters event rarely needs to see the crowd warmed up, even less when it compiles the cream of both the female and male crops. Add one of its own to the mix – Spaniard David Ferrer from Valencia, ending his own impressive career there – and you have the ingredients for something special, even more than previous years.

It's a testament to what Ferrer has achieved – his character and his eternal ability to battle, outfight and keep going – that this feels like a big loss to the game and that he is being bid a fond farewell. He is making his final appearances in the early months of 2019, and continues to discard his headband (post-defeat) at each tournament, where the deuce and advantage service boxes meet the service line. It was all leading up to this; ending things at the largest event Spain hosts in the ATP calendar year. Seeing him in Barcelona, recently, only served to demonstrate just how compelling an on-court character the man has been. Faced with the task of beating Nadal on clay again, he didn't shrink away, he didn't cower, he took him on, and for the most part represented himself well. Let us not forget that he is now 37. And for a normal human being – a non-Federer one – it is normal to accept one's physical decline by now, and hang up one's tennis shoes.

It Feels Like a Slam

The Madrid Open (like the Indian Wells and Miami Opens before it in the calendar year) feels like a Slam. Some of the players say it, the quality of the draw speaks of it, and as a spectator it has the feel of a big tournament; everyone is hungry to do some damage on a big platform and leave their footprints all over the clay of the Spanish capital.

The quality is high, the early match-ups of the week are often electric, and it's one week (unlike in Indian Wells and Miami where events are stretched out, including qualifying, to around two weeks) that's jam-packed with almost endless action, not to mention the doubles' events and so on. It's hard to tear your eyes from; no sooner does one day end, with play until late, than its successor appears – a spring banquet for all involved.

When the Two Tours Collide

Something feels complete when both the women and the men converge on a tennis tournament at the same time. It feels like it matters, like it's capable of hosting a plethora of brilliant matches across the genders in the singles, doubles, and girls and boys draws. Quite simply, on the face of it, it's magnificent. After many events that are either for the women or the men, well, this has a magic that's absent elsewhere. Another tournament closer to a Grand Slam, everyone scrambling and starving for form, full of vibrating bodies of intense anticipation and speculation as the conclusion – Roland Garros itself – draws nearer.

The two tours complement one another, just as women and men do in general life.

There is a buzz, a continuity, a feeling that everything is in its right place. While perhaps it wouldn't work to the same effect on a permanent basis – although I would love to see it attempted – you cannot help but feel the impact of the two tours colliding like comets; they seem destined to be together.

Kvitová Defeats Mladenovic (Madrid Open, 2nd Round)

It's a tie-break in set two between Kiki Mladenovic and Petra Kvitová, and the first eight points had been mini-breaks. Mladenovic then wins a service point to lead 5-4, and Kvitová follows suit bringing some normalcy back to proceedings. The Czech then wins the next two points (making up a strange complexion to the tie-break), to win the match and make round three, winning 6-3, 7-6.

Petra is in the form of her life. Her eyes are perhaps not fixed on the top mantle – the number one ranking – but her body is heading in that direction regardless. Barring Osaka's sublime ascent to the top, few other women are revealing themselves to be genuine contenders for the perch of the WTA rankings and Kvitová, a couple of years on from her worst ordeal, is finding some consistently good form and looking a challenge on any surface. Petra's remarkable desire and her screeches and squeals of joy are lighting up the WTA and she is saying, while nobody else seems to be staking a claim on the top of the ladies' game – perhaps apart from Osaka – that she is here, and she wants it. The glory, the championships, and the spotlight that come with it, all of it. She works hard and lets her tennis do the talking. She is the ultimate model for what a tennis player should be, and how they should carry themselves, both on and off the court. A graceful modern icon.

Ashleigh Barty's Tennis Brain

The on-court IQ of Ashleigh Barty is a phenomenal sporting characteristic, a feature that has now propelled the young Australian into the WTA top 10 for the first time in her career, in recent months. She's one of the true thinkers of the sport, with a feel and touch to match (a rarity if truth be told), and she is also one of the most delightful presences in the locker room – that's what the other players say. Her on-court interviews further support what a down to earth and focussed young lady she really is.

A consummate professional, clearly a hard worker and a mature, dedicated, and incredibly likeable lady, don't be surprised to see her lodged in the top ten for a long time now. She's one of those players who takes and learns her lessons well and uses them to her advantage – ever-improving and growing as a player – aware of the grander scheme of things in the career of a sportsperson. She's also one of those players nobody wants to be drawn against early in a tournament, and the longer she stays in an event – the more lethal she becomes.

The Double Bagel – A Dish Only Served Cold

There's no way to enjoy being on the receiving end of a double bagel. Rather, it's best to use it as the ultimate learning experience from someone who has evidently mastered the challenge of tennis to a larger degree. With the knowledge that none of us has ever perfected an art form, however close to that we may think we have come, then we will continue to learn and evolve as we indeed should.

While the baker of the bagels is on fire, the recipient is cold as ice – frozen, statuesque, and left reeling inside. They wish they could've found a better version of themselves – or a magic formula to combat the onslaught with – and offered a better display of their abilities. Sometimes it isn't even close. That's just life.

The David Ferrer Swansong Files

And so... the script dictates that David Ferrer's first-round match in Madrid against compatriot Roberto Bautista Agut will go to a deciding set. Ferrer won the first, his serve failed him somewhat in set two, and here we stand – perhaps on the cusp of Ferrer's final ever set of professional tennis. Either way, that final set will take place at some point, this week, that fate has pencilled it in for.

Ferrer breaks at the start of set three and, at 2-1, something happens at the start of the following game. Bautista Agut makes a drop shot, Ferrer just gets it before the second bounce and is then awarded the point he goes on to win. Bautista Agut questions the call from the drop shot return, and Ferrer – in extraordinarily gentlemanly fashion – offers to replay the point. The umpire had given the point to Ferrer, but his opponent had questioned the call, and he displayed striking sportsmanship. He proceeded to win the replayed point but is then broken back. 2-2.

The atmosphere is palpable. The crowd willing Ferrer to glory. Although Bautista Agut *might* ordinarily win a meeting between the pair in 2019, the sense of occasion is huge for both men, as well as the crowd inside and outside of the arena, and this is a special and unique moment. The crowd 'gets it' and the two men start playing more tentative shots, locked and lost inside the moment, framing these magical scenes on court – a match that will be remembered either way, but particularly if Bautista Agut prevails. Ferrer breaks again and, with no signs of pain or discomfort, takes a medical time out to have some work done on his left thigh. Hopefully, he will be okay to continue, leading 3-2 in the final set as he is doing.

And the silence when Ferrer loses points is deadly, cutting like a murderous knife. Everyone is teetering on the brink here, not to mention the players. Ferrer may have to play through the soreness here to survive to live another day. He is going to have to find that magic of his from somewhere. He is broken again. 3-3.

Ferrer breaks yet again! This match is the ultimate three-set rollercoaster ride. Ferrer fails when he has two break points at 15-40. Then Bautista Agut can't take his one game point, either, and Ferrer takes the third chance shown to him, at advantage this time. He then leads 4-3. He absolutely must hold his serve. The ambience is frightening as everyone (less Bautista Agut's camp) seems to be willing Ferrer to find the key to unlock one more match victory. Always one more. The dream alive.

Ferrer then finally holds. To love, to boot. More than to love, he holds his serve for a 5-3 lead. It's in his hands. It's on his racket. It's a whisper away.

Bautista Agut serves well, holds relatively easily, and passes the service baton to his Spanish teammate of the past.

Ferrer has two match points, loses both, then wins at deuce for a third shot at sealing an impressive deal. He then manages to find a way through the wall of Bautista Agut and claims what might be the final victory of his career, for who knows what lies in wait just around the corner.

It was not easy, today, for Bautista Agut, but he also battled and made a real match of it. A mark of his own character (after the Murray episode in Melbourne in January just gone, he may have had enough of these heavily-nuanced matches), but for most people, this has been and will continue to be about Ferrer while he continues to draw breath on the court at the Madrid Open. Alex Zverev, not in great form of late and defending his title, is in for a genuinely uncomfortable ride tomorrow in front of a partisan crowd. The Ferrer fairy-tale rolls into the next round like a Mardi Gras parade float, all eyes fixed right this way...

David Ferrer is seventh on the list of active players in terms of win/loss % on clay. Thiem is ahead, along with the top three of Nadal, Djokovic, and Federer, and Del Potro and Nishikori are above Ferrer but also on 71%. The actual 'matches won' list has Ferrer second behind only Nadal. Ferrer with 334 wins on clay to his 139 losses; they are extraordinary stats that show just what a force he has proven to be on the surface, over his almost two-decade professional career.

In match number 1,111 of his career, he today faces Alexander Zverev who he has already beaten this year. It won't be a given that the young seed will be the conqueror, and eject Ferrer into his retirement. Zverev's form of late suggests he won't echo his title success here in Madrid from last year. Form doesn't, however, always hold true. Zverev may want to avoid irking what will be a totally biased crowd. Forget that Zverev holds this title, it's in Spain, it may be Ferrer's last ever professional match, and, well, do we need more than that? What more is there?

Ferrer to serve first. He trails the pair's head-to-head by 3-4. It'd be wonderful to draw level in their final match ever, I bet. He tucks the first game (to thirty) into his pocket, the players change ends and go again. Two service games to love then follow, which settles the players.

Zverev service game, 30-40, here we go... Ferrer does break, or rather is gifted the game with a Zverev double fault, much to the entire arena's supporting voice and applause.

Ferrer (and his army of fans; a legion) is starting to annoy Zverev. It doesn't take much to wind up the towering

German and if Ferrer carries on playing like this, Zverev will surely contribute to his own undoing. Ferrer has his best battle-gear on and, late in the day, this is not a match Zverev will be enjoying one second of. Does he have the guts to go toe to toe with a legend of the sport in his final moments? Power, grace, lob, drop shot, you name it, Ferrer uses it to hold and take the next game and a 4-1 first set lead. Ferrer's hunger, coupled with the crowd and Zverev's ability to shoot himself in the foot, is making it easy so far.

Zverev wins the next two games, and the feel of 4-3 at the next changeover has an entirely different complexion. Ferrer sees Zverev to deuce on serve, pushing every button he can to find a way to win the set. This is exactly why he is so loved, revered, why everybody wants more of him. He can't manage to find a way and it's level at 4-4, a real stern test for both men now.

Zverev breaks again, realising he doesn't have to participate in the party the way others want him to, when Ferrer had been 30-0 up. And now it's all to do for the Spaniard in this first set. Ferrer throws his very essence, more than the proverbial kitchen sink, at Zverev, but he holds serve for the opening set. The kitchen sink has landed on Zverev's side of the court, another thing against him, and he has stood up, taken the assault and found a solution to this late-night Madrid puzzle. It's a challenge of some magnitude. All to do for Ferru! *Vamos, Ferru!* (as the crowd shouts Ferrer's nickname endlessly into the Spanish night).

At the start of set two, Ferrer is broken again, and it's a sad sign of what is to come. He hasn't won a game since he led 4-1 a little while back. Zverev has focused, got his head down in difficult conditions, and worked his way through a minefield. It's now in his hands. Or is it? Zverev doesn't want to lose the ranking points that would come with a second-round loss here. He doesn't want to be undone by the Spanish spectators, nor by their man in his final ever match. The ending looms larger by the minute, but the cheers for Ferrer's point wins – the love and adoration he receives – are abundantly clear. Ferrer is then 40-0 down on Zverev's serve. He gets it back to deuce, in complete control of the rallies that get beyond nine shots in length, grinding down his opposition as has done to so many opponents. But, despite this, it goes to 2-0 in the second; Ferrer has a German mountain in front of him on this late spring night in Madrid.

Zverev has Ferrer on the ropes now, a demolition taking place. It's a shame Zverev saved a return to form for this match, and this rival, on this specific day. But such is life. Ferrer has now lost eight games in a row as the scoreboard shows 3-0.

Time is almost up.

Three becomes four and Ferrer has yet to get a game this set. It's a valiant effort, but it's simply time to head off into the sunset. And he deserves a magical moment. He has been a warrior like very few in the history of the sport and, while he hasn't won any majors, he has been one of the male tennis voices of a generation, and a combatant that showed you didn't need huge weapons if you had grit and determination and an endless well of passion for the sport. A humble guy, to boot, his work ethic was second to none.

Ferrer finally gets on the board this set. 1-4. Then he trails 1-5 as Zverev holds serve. Ferrer faces his possible final game of a tennis match in his professional career. Serving to stay in the job...

He looks tired, like all the years on-court have now – finally – caught up. 0-30. 0-40 on a double fault. Now standing on the precipice. A standing ovation breaks out for Ferrer, who is unable to serve. The noise. The emotion of it all. It's hit long from the racket of Ferrer when the point finally does get under way.

It's over.

Then comes the earthquake of noise for him, the match loser but today's winner. Zverev is mostly forgotten as the tribute to David Ferrer flows.

Ferrer radiates warmth towards the crowd. So many stories, and more to tell soon, no doubt. Twenty-seven titles in his career. A Masters title in Paris, Bercy. He stays on court to take the plaudits and the adoring public rightly worships him for half an hour or so, showing what he means to them. It's an end to a wonderful career. 'Gracias Ferru' says the banner they unfurl at the back of the court. He looks proud and overwhelmed. Camera people are everywhere. His wife and young son join him on the court, and they bask in the spotlight. A video of career highlights is played, with snippets of players sending messages, comments, and love.

"We're going to miss you, that's the truth!" says Nadal, in Spanish, at the end of the video. Succinctly put. Accurate, too.

Ferrer makes his mother cry with the words he dedicates to his parents. He then says the last ten years have been the best because of having his wife at his side – and he teases tears from her eyes, too. Ferrer bows out with grace and great shared warmth. A peak of the year's many fine moments so far (and surely come the end as well).

A day or so later, Ferrer would write a note to the world of tennis and the younger players out there. He would – in one paragraph – capture his very essence; one that youngsters and pros and amateurs alike would love to take to the court with them.

"Everyone has to pursue their own path and a way of working out things. In my case, at the end, what I learned is that normally you learn from defeats, from the losses, the tough moments, because you have to miss a lot of time, you have to taste defeat, you have to stand up and continue and keep on working. That was what was driving me to be the tennis player that I am today. And to accept the tough and frustrating moments and face them and recover. And to pursue your dreams, but not one or two, or three days, but you have to do it all of your career. I would like to always be remembered for my personality, the way I am personally. I think I am a good person to the very last day of my existence."

The Return of Stan the Man
(Madrid Open)

Some of Stanislas Wawrinka's tennis, in his win over Kei Nishikori, is as good as he has played in some time. Even years. Not only today, but this week he has announced himself... the return! What else could it be called? And he looks like he means business. Nishikori is no pushover on clay; see his titles and close battles of yore on the surface.

You cannot find yourself on a Grand Slam winner's platform based on fortune; those events are far too demanding in multiple ways. To win multiple Slams in the age of arguably the best three male tennis players – ever – is an achievement that warrants praise.

Wawrinka has had his injuries, has come across as surly and less approachable than some of the top guys, but he has carved out his own space and done things on his own terms. Indeed, he has done things that other top players (with no Slams) will look at with great envy. Now, at 34, he looks fresh and ready to make something big happen again, or at least give it a whirl. With the last two years spent either injured, recovering from injury, or slowly and steadily clawing his way along the comeback trail, this week represents a time to mark him as a handful for anyone he faces over the coming weeks. Let's face it, he absolutely adores that dark horse status; he's traveling through the draw in Swiss stealth fashion.

Osaka v Bencic
(Madrid Open, Quarter-Final)

Otherwise known as the 'battle of the young divas', this ladies' quarter-final has it all. Both women are throwing and dropping rackets, mumbling, complaining, and talking to themselves and their teams (indeed, anyone who might help them out of their respective messes). Both women are remarkably talented, and have grown up in the spotlight. They lack humility, and a dose of that might help to deliver them to reality whilst being global superstars (well, Bencic is well on her way, Osaka cannot avoid it as world number one).

Women's tennis is remarkably rich right now, but it does not pull people in when the players involved act like spoilt madams.

Osaka loses 6-3, 2-6, 5-7. As good as Bencic is, you cannot help but feel the outcome was shaped by Osaka's later confession that thinking about the number one ranking affected her match. The honesty is refreshing, but why on earth? Clearly, the ranking matters, and is on her mind whilst playing a professional match. The admission is a rather incredible window into the young and brilliant world of the Japanese tennis player, and how her mind ticks.

The Federer Effect

How many more players are going to lose to Federer's reputation rather than beat the man in front of them? These players seem wholly able to beat the legend until they subsequently work their way into a corner from which they will not emerge unscathed. They are keeping him in a job, seemingly nobody wanting to retire him from the sport.

Do not get me wrong. He is still brilliant and more than capable, on his day, of beating just about any player out there. It just often seems, lately, that he is winning matches he should not be. While age isn't doing and hasn't done the same damage to a man who glides rather than runs, and who floats rather than skids, he is being helped to extend a career through sheer fear of his greatness. Serena, on the ladies' side of things is equally (though in an altogether separate approach), able to induce fear and uncertainty in her opponents, too – forcing them into self-doubt and error-strewn games that might not normally occur. And then comes the pounce. As the greats do, they smell fear and launch themselves upon their prey. It's all over then, even before the final outcome appears.

Roger Federer and Serena Williams will both look back on their later years and know their shadows – the shape and size of them – to be factors in how they survived. Their shadows helped them win when perhaps things shouldn't have quite turned out that way.

Bringing us back to today, Gael Monfils had the legend's scalp there for the taking, in his hands. With several match points that he failed to convert, Monfils joins the others this year who came close but got no cigar. Bottling it at key moments is not something new for Gael, either. Federer knows he is fortunate, but at the same time, he is making it happen when those players are not. He is hanging in and deserving of the fruits of his persistent labour. That cannot be argued. As for those on the losing end, it's a lesson and something to inevitably rue come the day's inevitable reflection.

Federer is a great who will not see his ranking slide nor succumb to endless losses; he won't allow it. He won't go out on a crash, more like a bang – the right moment mercilessly calculated as much of his career has been. When he starts to lose more regularly, he will quit the sport. He doesn't love it *that* much. But matches he shouldn't really be winning, his endless experience and savvy, and, of course, his reputation which follows him everywhere, are enabling him to keep the (arguably not so express) train to match wins, and even tournament victories (two this year). Kudos, Roger.

Bertens Rising

For those whose preferred surface is clay, this is the time of the year to cash in on that. Kiki Bertens is a player who seems to improve year on year, quietly climbing the rankings in extremely admirable fashion, every rung upwards is a validation of hard work and endeavour.

Here in Madrid, she didn't so much beat the in-form Kvitova as destroy her – once again showing her red dirt game to be the one she loves the most. Bertens is continuing to do her thing under the radar, which seems to be to her liking. It's as though the tennis gods are asking, 'how high can you get in the rankings before the world notices you?' Well, while others certainly demand the limelight more, it goes a long way to state that playing tennis and doing so well is what really counts.

Roger Federer, Master of Instinct

Federer's army of fans is there for a reason. Watch him on court, and you are guaranteed – whether he is *on it*, or not – to see impulses and instincts that display a ferociously natural talent, a man who has an all-seeing eye for the sport, and who enhances it with his shots. The outrageous never looked so within someone's easy range of skills; scarcely seemed so fluid and on tap. There's a deep well for the artist himself, the Swiss man.

Some of Roger's speed and effortlessness on the ball and the shot-making, from his ageing hands, were as impressive as I've ever seen from him. He hadn't played the clay court season since 2016, making his run at this week's Madrid Open even more impressive. Yesterday, he didn't present his best self in sets two and three (despite winning against Monfils), and looked far from his finest. Aside from the first set yesterday (a bagel), he again didn't look great but he turned that form around today with a great display of his poetic abilities.

Today he may have lost in the Madrid semi-final, but he pushed Dominic Thiem all the way, a man who is capable of beating Rafa on this surface (and who did so only a few weeks earlier). He played some tennis that didn't seem possible – okay, so nothing new – but as time goes by, the joy of still witnessing Federer reach fresh peaks, of playing at his vicious best, is overwhelmingly powerful. Knowing at what age and in what state many of the past legends of the sport began to decline at, and hang up their rackets at, it seems even more miraculous that he refuses to fade away. There's no denying that even on such days, most other players in the world will be wondering what on earth can be done against that type of tennis.

The Honorary Madrileña

It's not easy to predict a winner on the ladies' side when contemplating what lies ahead over the first weekend of the Madrid Open (it stretches over an extended week, encompassing two weekends), but several players emerge as obvious ones-to-watch. Perhaps none more so than some of the usual suspects: Simona Halep, Naomi Osaka, and Petra Kvitová (the latter two looking unusually good on clay as players figure it out at various stages of their respective careers). Only one can take home the silverware and in the end, this year's honorary *Madrileña* is Kiki Bertens, whose form goes from strength to strength, now lodged (as she is) inside the world's top ten. All kinds of Dutch class and technique are her forte and beating Halep in straight sets – 6-4, 6-4 – only goes to cement her status as one of the favourites for the imminent Roland Garros title. Her on-court days look increasingly impressive.

Nadal Betters Djokovic
(Rome Open Final)

There can be no denying it. That must feel good to the Spaniard – given what has come before this clay court season. With the imminent arrival of another Roland Garros, Nadal will feel confident and will undoubtedly take the plunge to find another title, a twelfth.

What better test, right before the dawn of a new Grand Slam – his favourite by far – which you would hope and expect to win, than that of the world number one and perennial Serbian nemesis, Novak Djokovic. The perfect way of measuring one's renewed form, of probing one's own boundaries of comfort and manageability, of discovering how close you are to your best.

Rafael Nadal, on this occasion, beats Novak Djokovic and claims yet another Masters title on clay – the Rome Open – with the odd line of 6-0, 4-6, 6-1. The topsy-turvy sets show that Djokovic can find a way to break, and hurt Nadal, but that if he finds his killer groove, Nadal is impossible to match on clay. Even after all these years. While such results seldom mean too much come Grand Slam showdowns (a totally different kettle of fish in all their epic potential five-set glories), it can only bolster the confidence levels of the Spaniard. A man who has clearly been struggling of late, wrestling with his body and the mental effects of carrying around the memories of recent injury turmoil and the clay court losses – the added anticipation of always imminent injury –in the aftermath of his latest unfortunate withdrawal at Indian Wells. It cannot be easy and thus far, going into the big one; he has kept his head held high and reacted admirably to recent defeats in the semi-finals of the events in Monte Carlo, Barcelona, and Madrid, some of his most successful stamping grounds to date. Ultimately, this win feels like opening the door to another Roland Garros title – an opening that just didn't look as likely in recent weeks.

ROLAND GARROS: A BALLET

Clay Kicks Up

More than any other surface (grass gives it a go), clay wants to go with the players, wants to allow them to leave their marks. When those same bodies launch into the air from the service motion and other spellbinding shots, the clay attempts to reach up, to follow, to shadow the players as they move. The dance between the two is exotic and entrancing, like no other in the sport.

It's still early. Pre-noon. The seats haven't been filled yet as the women do battle. A top player and an unknown (to most, still, perhaps not for much longer). Round one. Early tensions and frustrations mirrored by calm and fluidity. No mirror of choice to the underdog, struggling to hold serve, to find a game that keeps a first-set bagel at bay.

Switching between the courts, there are some wonderful encounters for the first round. Some are tight and some are one-sided. Some blossom and others wilt. And as the calmness is replaced by rustling bodies and louder noise, the young woman who was being well-beaten turns the match around and wins in three (detailed below). The seed is defeated, the underdog smiles and looks towards the next round, basking in the first singles victory on Court Philippe Chatrier this year.

Veronika Kudermetova is rising up the rankings. Now at WTA number 68, having started the year outside the top 100, she finds herself on the chief court of Roland Garros' red clay (on the first Monday). The young Russian, a little 'deer in the headlights' early on, soon settled and found her groove against past Grand Slam winner, Caroline Wozniacki.

After a bagel in the opening set, Kudermetova finally wakes up and comes to the party. The Russian breaks Wozniacki twice in set two, leads 4-1, gets broken back, once, and collars the set by six games to three. In set three, the youngster continues to wind up Wozniacki, who starts to look like letting it all out, setting loose her rage.

In the final set, Kudermetova looks the part and is showing why she has seen a ranking surge this year and is worthy of a spot in a Slam. She breaks to hold the advantage. Wozniacki breaks back, then oddly surrenders her next service game. Kudermetova holds and is three games ahead, giving her three shots at a hugely unlikely win. And it all started with that bagel in the first set. What a stunning turnaround it is as she claims the win.

Nadal does what is expected of him and dispatches the qualifier, world number 180, Yannick Hanfmann, in straight sets. It's no surprise that he speeds ahead, no shock it's over quickly.

More madness as Medvedev goes two up, then gets pegged back at 2-2 by Pierre-Hughes Herbert. The final set causes a real stormy scene as it's neck and neck in the decider. The crowd is clearly with Herbert, the Frenchman, who finally breaks for 6-5 and then serves it out to wild applause and joy. An unlikely comeback, a mad partisan crowd, and a helping hand thoroughly enjoyed by Herbert. A backward step for Medvedev? We shall see.

A Love Letter to the Five-Set Format

Dear Five-Set Format

You have provided us with endless enchantment. You have been questioned and you have fought back, shown what you are made of, spun a web of delight over many, capturing and conquering.

We've been here before, under threat and apprehensive and then you turn up, spill the goods and remind them of just why you prevail. Only at the majors, a feast of the slams, a facet of incomparable joy. The rest of the year, the remainder of events see three sets and short-lived brilliance, but the slams demand something else, construct edifices of value and beauty unparalleled.

The thrillers are coming thick and fast. Day four, the first day of round two. Herbert signals himself a true hero – with Jo-Wilfried Tsonga losing today and Richard Gasquet yesterday – as he approaches a second comeback in three days from two sets behind. This time fellow Frenchman Benoit Paire stops him in his tracks at the very last. Herbert loses 11-9 in the final set. At 7-7 in the final set (his tenth set in the singles since Monday), he has his chances and fails, watching it all vanish rather than materialise. Grigor Dimitrov comes from 2-1 down in sets to beat Marin Čilić in an epic over four sets. Filip Krajinović and Roberto Carballes Baena also exchange a marathon. We may well be left exhausted, but without any desire to change what is sheer tennis perfection.

Long live the five-set format!

Paire v Herbert (Round 2)

The Benoit Paire drop shot to bring up match point is otherworldly. Some of the droppers this week have been as sublime as ever, showing how gifted the hands of the elite are.

Paire looks exhausted, overwhelmed; perhaps he didn't expect this – a final set where he had led by two sets to love. Or possibly he had accessed his well of sympathy for his compatriot, not put the fighter to the sword, and then been entrenched in an increasingly demanding match. For the shattered look on Paire's face, Herbert displays abject deflation. What a finale though. 11-9 to Paire in the final set. A place in round three (where there are only 32 players left lining up).

Today's match was over four and a half hours of true Parisian magic, shared between two Frenchmen. The hug at the end, heartfelt, the words exchanged, the sense of meaning, the weight, the audience response, feeding off the court's antics. A highlight of the tournament so far, if not THE highlight. Pure wonder. The Grand Slams keep on giving and Paris' appetite is sated once more by its own.

Eyes on Markéta Vondroušová

Eyes on a teenager again, this time Czech soon-to-be-sensation Markéta Vondroušová. It's a name to put a star against, as she rises looking to achieve great altitude before she hits her twenties. Something like Ostapenko, she is a real threat and with growing confidence; the kind that makes youth lethal at times. She will be a tough task for anyone facing her across the net this fortnight.

The more I see of young Vondroušová, the more I like her. An approach that is workwomanlike, incredibly focussed, and beyond her years, she is one of the up-and-comers who demands less off-court attention but whose tennis is taking giant strides. They are leaps and bounds propelling her towards the top.

Today, in the second round, she faces the slightly younger Russian, Anastasia Potapova (who turned 18 in March; you may remember her from winning the Wimbledon Juniors three years ago), world number 81. Vondroušová is ranked 38 and will herself turn 20 next month just before Wimbledon. Her form this year reflects a woman on the rise, not wanting to wait on any of the great things that evidently await her.

Vondroušová is soon 4-1 down though her engine gets started, and it all soon clicks into gear. She draws level at four games apiece and then breaks again to serve for the opening set. She does indeed do that, winning five games on the trot by the close of the opener.

Potapova's game implodes, and she loses her first two service games of set two for her Czech rival to now lead 6-4, 3-0. Three becomes five all too easily, which in turn becomes six and puts the match to bed early in what became a total demolition of the younger player. Potapova will have nightmares, whilst Vondroušová will relish the third-round meeting with Spaniard, Carla Suarez Navarro, just getting going as the young Czech player is.

Vondroušová, with this performance, current form, and her stealth Czech approach has earmarked herself as a dark young horse looking for a deep run at the title, if not claiming the silverware. She has nothing to lose, all to gain, and has the game and the growing confidence to make a mark. Keep your eyes peeled!

Lucie Šafářová Exits the Game

Fresh from the loss of David Ferrer, another brilliant player this side of the millennium has retired. This time it is Czech doubles specialist and multiple Grand Slam doubles winning titlist and on-her-day a singles wizard who climbed to a WTA career-high singles ranking of five in the world: Lucie Šafářová. She was the runner up in Paris in 2015 to Serena Williams and winner of five doubles majors. The lady has certainly left her mark on the women's game. She held the doubles world number one ranking for six weeks back in 2017, achieving great heights and punching at one hell of a weight in both singles and doubles simultaneously; a feat few could truly manage nowadays.

Thirty-two seems like a young age at which to head off into the sunset, but with what she managed to accomplish across the singles, doubles, and team competitions, she has more than filled her career. Over a jam-packed decade-plus, she amassed shelves and shelves full of memories, and can happily move on to the next phase of her career and life.

Lucie Šafářová, like others before her, was awarded a special commemorative gift, hers a memento of some of the Roland Garros court surface in a tidy Perspex casing, emblazoned with her name and a 'thank you!', to remind her of her time at the event. A place in which she had seen some of her greatest successes and, as she would state, which was her favourite tournament.

A Late-Night Finish

Filip Krajinović asks to play on; Stefanos Tsitsipas would prefer to stop. The former is closing in on the set. He can take it now; hence his desire to continue as the day darkens and visibility is reduced. They do play on. It's ten to ten at night. Light is fading dramatically, meaning the soap opera of the evening is hitting its climax. Krajinović serves at 5-3, and it's 30-30.

A little while ago, elsewhere, Stanislas Wawrinka had taken the second set on a tie-break over Grigor Dimitrov, to lead by two sets to love – echoing the way he had closed out the first set.

Krajinović surrenders his first chance to take the math to a fourth set, with Tsitsipas two sets to love up as it stands, and – oddly – as night engulfs those involved, they keep playing. While the drama is compelling, it's utterly strange that they keep going, that someone has made that decision. Eleven hours after play at Roland Garros started, it's still happening. 5-5. Play finally ends there for the day. To a small chorus of boos. The crowd had been lucky; there are no floodlights, and tennis in the dark hasn't become a sport. Yet.

A near ten o'clock finish. As brilliant as it has been, there are more than enough courts to easily finish the singles each day. That every day has matches carried over from the one before is something to irk fans and players alike, surely.

Advantage Serena

Whether she is still in a draw or not, you cannot help but focus your attention, at times, to the greats of the game. Serena Williams is one such player. I've been contemplating the 'Serena Effect', most certainly an actual thing, an event, an occurrence – possibly even a living entity – a beast that attacked other players and rendered them immobile.

Advantage Serena. It's with her before she and her opponent take to the court on any given day. A little like Rafa, she exerts a sense of fear and failing upon those she challenges; many of the younger players are daunted and are running scared from the offset.

It's a quality few have ever had, and those who had it (and knew how to wield it), such as Navratilova, Graf, Federer and Nadal, well, they are some of the best-known tennis players ever, regularly lighting up those well-known stages with the consistent and the mind-blowing.

Point

A serve comes down, is met by a flicked wrist, a diver's move – racket strings meeting to re-send – to deliver the ball back to where it came from. A chase, an arm extended, the body and its muscles contorting, a defensive wall positioned by one, as the attack comes in waves – ferocious, bitter, irresistible. You can taste the ball almost launched down your throat. This task I take on. It gets heavier. The wall, a forcefield. Not enough. More than cracks in that armour, everything you have built tumbles around you, falls like a flutter of leaves as the damage is inflicted, done and felt, beyond repair.

The blood is flowing, the veins are pulsating, the courage of all kinds of hearts.

A microcosm of everything, of all you find to have meaning. The love, the passion, the focus, the straining to achieve. How you approach one single point might just express what you can achieve on a much grander scale. It is the character with which a castle is built.

Middle Sunday Epic

Stanislas Wawrinka is walking the tightrope in set two with his one-set lead over Stefanos Tsitsipas. Stan is set point down with a drop shot from nowhere that crawls over the net to win the point. Narrow margins calling. The crowd is behind him, a former winner; a man with a rather unique personality, Tsitsipas is getting angry, violent, showing how bad he can be at losing.

Characters fray as temperatures rise to boiling point. Tsitsipas is not one for behaving admirably when locked in fierce battle and not getting it all his own way.

Five hours and nine minutes it takes. Stan had saved all seven break points he had faced – across three different service games – in the final set, meeting the challenge of those biggest points head on. No fear. The words of his tattoo – the Samuel Beckett quote "Ever tried. Ever failed. No matter. Try Again. Fail again. Fail better" – ringing loud in his ears, afraid of nothing, life and its lessons, echoing forever. Wawrinka claims the final set 8-6. The match of the fortnight so far, and it might be a tough one to top.

Match point was won; it was in by a millimetre. A massive effort from both men, an incredible match, and somehow sad that someone had to lose it. Yes, one of those! One for the ages, one that left an imprint on the consciousness.

Missing Muguruza

Muguruza has gone missing at the top; her attitude seemingly getting in the way.

She expects, she assumes, she underestimates the other women; she takes her past glories and wonders why they do not deliver more. In professional sport, nothing is a given. You must reset each and every time, and 'go again' as sports folks often state. Look at your compatriot, Nadal, and your fellow singles winner of Wimbledon 2017, a certain Mr Federer. Look closely and you will see that whenever they won, they took each opponent seriously and gave their best; their longevity is testament to this too as nobody, and nothing, can be taken for granted.

On the face of it, does Muguruza really see one match, one round, one opponent at a time? It seems not. Instead, it seems like she thinks of the bigger picture, and her known ability to win majors. That mindset is what's holding her back, pulling her even further away from the greatness that was possibly her destiny. The cards tell a wholly different story as endless special talents appear as if from nowhere (like the shopkeeper in the kid's TV program Mr. Benn – you'll either know this reference or not).

Muguruza's rival today, Sloane Stephens, has a wonderfully focussed on-court demeanour; it stays strong and unbroken by crowds and losing points, games and sets. She's a bright spark that knows how to carry herself on the big stages on which more and more divas are acting up and getting down. For many, self-applied pressure (or is it inflicted by others?) is too much to handle.

No expression on Stephens' face, even when she faces break points and meets with difficulties when serving for the match; things are occurring under the surface, hidden, unrevealing. She is a picture of calmness and concentration, a peaceful player to watch. She merits the straight sets win and looks good as the players head towards the final rounds. She outplays Muguruza today – both women Grand Slam champions – and is now becoming rather consistent at the French Open. Stephens is an ongoing force to be reckoned with.

Set the Bar High

Markéta Vondroušová, in her stellar Grand Slam breakthrough, demolishes Anastasia Sevastova on Court Suzanne Lenglen to the point of sending her to another court, even another planet.

Vondroušová wins so comprehensively, it's hard to believe her age, that she hasn't done *this* before, and that she isn't at (or very near) the top of the game already. It's a mature performance, and if the young Czech had not already caught people's eyes, then surely this was the one to do that. Her name has appeared more and more this year and, rather than waiting to clock up a few more years, Vondroušová has jumped through the open doorway and said 'why not now?' with her tennis.

No one woman is seizing the game by the scruff of its neck, though Osaka at world number one and with two first Slams pocketed back-to-back is as close as anyone has come in that regard. To what extent she is there to stay will become evident in the coming months and years, as the pressure to sustain wins and hold form becomes harder.

Others remaining in the draw – going into the quarter-final stage – might beware, as the young Czech looks an authentic threat. With nothing to fear, her status resembles that of Ostapenko two years back. Playing higher-ranked players will certainly be the true measuring stick of where Vondroušová is, but the way she grows with every match makes her one of those few players who it's hard to get enough of. Surely she is a player to love and follow to the ends of the earth? Another comparison with the Ostapenko of 2017 is that this late teenager seems to have no anxiety and looks like she enjoys the thrill of destroying others on court, an act that surely becomes addictive the more one tastes its salty goodness.

Vondroušová can reach almost everything. She has demolished the will of her rival today and looks like she moves around the court like a female Tsitsipas, or even Federer, not that such comparisons are reasonable... but everybody always seems to want them), Her court coverage and angles remind me of Djokovic. Young female players like this are worthy of our full attention as much as any male, and the fact that the stands were part empty for this one-hour lesson dished out by a mere teenager to a seasoned pro, is a disgrace. Tennis continues to grow as a sport, yet it feels like it's reaching the wrong people.

Tennis is, too often, an elite sport; a creation of the wealthy masses that still veers clear of poorer folks who might love to play and watch the sport. It would be a shame if they didn't get the chance to sit in front of young players like Vondroušová at some point in her career, or even to become the next one like her. Open your gates, make it more than a dream, fill the seats like other events do.

Vondroušová had already won around 20 matches this season before heading into Paris. That generally symbolises deep runs and great form, pushing a player ever higher up the rankings. It also depicts confidence, form, and ability – it's hard to fluke consistency. Well, it's nigh on impossible. She looks very, very good at this French Open, and while she hasn't played a top tenner yet, these are indeed significant strides.

Vondroušová is like a kid with an etch-a-sketch who has suddenly and surprisingly created something of beauty, making people take note. A work of art often comes from her racket these days. It looks effortless, as she floats and slides, and explores the different shots. With her tennis, she blows minds and all expectations out of the water, and into the stratosphere – another player we can expect to see a great deal more from over the coming months and years.

When the Sky Threatens

The dark, foreboding sky above Roland Garros, as the ladies' semi-finals take place, threatens to rain daggers down, to ruin it all, to swamp the fate of two women and – perhaps, if the rain doesn't skirt the site – two men as well. Rain from the day before had doomed the players and fans, and all involved.

The grey, the black, a gloomy net of gripping beauty, hovering, not wanting to leave, the backdrop slipping into the foreground. Rain will spill, and rain will splish-splash. It's a stunning sight as the dark heavens threaten to swallow Roland Garros, and everyone there, whole. It could have been painted by the brushes of Monet, Renoir, Turner, other greats. Nature, all around us, wheeling, circling, pondering its approach; an attack that is imminent.

Offset against the orange clay of the main courts at Roland Garros, the storm reflects a side of tennis, of life, of our personal and collective quests, that constant blue skies just don't accomplish. It brings a new shade, a fresh tinge to proceedings. No shadows glide; the players' hair and clothes and serves look different. We bask in what we love, framed completely unlike before; a brand new director helming these scenes of the film, bringing a vivid new life to it all.

The women's matches get started early, at 11am. Ashleigh Barty cruises into a 5-0 lead; the inharmonious weather entering Amanda Anisimova's world and crushing her. Anisimova then gets a break back to trail more respectably at 2-5. On the other side of the draw, Johanna Konta gets an early break over Markéta Vondroušová, and then a marathon fourth game of around ten minutes sees the young Czech break back for 2-2. All square, all to play for. The wind swirls and whips up the short tennis skirts as the players wait to serve and return; clay gets everywhere, a clay storm blowing all around. Anisimova gets back to 3-5. A real turn, after a brutally short first 15 minutes from Barty. Anisimova then has break points to level at 4-5, which she does. The weather is now playing havoc with the momentum of the matches – a ghost in the machines – with the desire to get on court, win, and get off without having rain delays. That rain may well define things, may help and hinder, may be a Holy Grail for some.

The clouds over the courts, and the fatal sweep of conditions, accompany the brushing of the court after each set. The Barty 5-0 lead, after a quarter of an hour, has now given way to being 5-6 down. A quite unexpected and breath-taking turnaround has taken place. It seemed impossible, let alone unlikely. The wind kicks up sporadically, the rain is halted, as though waiting for permission to deliver, desperate to pounce, like a liquid tiger throwing itself over the courts. And Konta leads by a break after getting it back earlier for 3-2. She now leads 5-3. Umpires are wearing coats and cardigans, the fans watching live, too.

Barty breaks and a tie-break follows. Meanwhile, Vondroušová is serving to stay in set one against Konta. Once there, Konta serves for the set, and is again broken for 5-5. Barty and Anisimova's tie-break seemed unlikely at 5-0 to Barty, and she will regret having not taken her set points earlier as the teenage American Anisimova takes the set on a breaker.

Rain is edging closer, now given the green light, and umbrellas start to go up. The court is swept to tidy up, ready for set two. Wild scenes both on and above the courts; amazing ladies' semi-final action, gripping to the last. With the strange set tied up between the Aussie Barty and American Anisimova, Vondroušová gets to 6-5 and breaks to take the opener over Konta, meaning that right now, the two teenagers each have one foot in the final.

In the second sets, Anisimova quickly wins three games running without losing a point. Barty holds serve; Anisimova serves at 3-1 up. Barty breaks, and oddly we are back on serve. After losing 17 points in a row, Barty gives herself a chance in the set and the match. While the kids have been yet another breath of fresh air in the women's game – and, boy, does it have an abundance of them – it wasn't a stretch to think the experience of their opponents today, Barty and Konta, might favour them in the semi-finals. With the youngsters both a set up, and Barty finding a way to level at 3-3, and Konta breaking Vondroušová in set two to lead, you cannot help but want these two matches to go the distance. Three sets of brilliance on the two respective courts that truly show what women's tennis is. These matches are far from over – plenty of ups and downs lurk, many unknown corners lie just up ahead.

Barty breaks and the pendulum has swung back again, 4-3 up, shortly after being 3-0 down. Barty has found her way out of the maze, and then goes 5-3 up. Konta holds over Vondroušová and leads 3-1. The tables have turned in both matches as if they are somehow psychically linked. Quick as you like, the comeback complete, and Barty makes it one set all after one hour and 14 minutes. Players blowing hot and cold like the weather this week. A final set ahead...

Konta leads by a break in set two. That match looks like it's heading for a final set, too. What a yo-yoing, rollercoaster match between Barty and Anisimova though. The two matches show, exactly, why the women's game is worth every inch what the men's is. That the women's tour doesn't achieve quite the attention the men's game does is endlessly frustrating. Vondroušová holds, meaning Konta will serve for the second set.

Barty is broken for an Anisimova 2-1 lead in the final set. The madness continues, but at least the weather hasn't encroached on things, and paused the action. Barty gets to three break points by swinging freely, releasing her demons, but fails to take any of them. Another chance at advantage and she claims this one! 2-2. On the other court, Konta serves for the second set, as she did in the first, and is broken. 5-5. She has had her chances for the match and not taken them. She will regret that when the teenage Czech is in the final. Vondroušová looks good now. Serves, takes the lead again for 6-5, and all the pressure is heaped on Konta once more. She must hold serve to stay in the tournament. She does, and we now have a second set tie-break.

Barty has broken Anisimova and leads 4-2; she now has it in her own hands to reach her first Roland Garros – and Grand Slam – final. Two games away. Eight points. It all sounds so easy, although based on this match, anything can still happen. Vondroušová is soon 2-0 up in the second set tie-break (with a mini-break), and she is only five points from that final tomorrow – also her first final of any Grand Slam. None of these four women has ever reached a Slam final, hence two battles of the ages for a pair of modern women's semis.

The wind and its clouds circle like vultures ready to dive down. Barty is 5-2 up, having served to be only a game away. 2019 tie-break records show Konta has won six and lost five, Vondroušová has won six out of six, meaning she is a player who excels at the biggest moments. There will be no third set, Vondroušová gets four match points and seals her slot in the final by taking the first one. Another teenager on fire in Paris, joyriding her way through the city's sporting highlight, hair tossed by the stormy wind, everything going her way.

Seconds later, Barty has three match points to meet Marketa Vondroušová there. She doesn't take the first. Nor the second. The third vanishes, too, Anisimova manages to hold; the wind's playing havoc with the final stages of women's semi-finals day. Barty will serve for it at 5-3. Here we go... the conditions, the rough and tumble of a young and free hitting opponent, the highs and lows, the rough with the smooth, it's an unfathomably exciting and wild day.

And Barty does do it! She takes her place in the final tomorrow. She comes back from a set and 3-0 down. Magical moments in a grey and almost miserable Paris. How can it be miserable when the tennis is *this* good? What a phenomenal couple of matches for the women's game and the whole world of tennis.

Barty and Anisimova both auditioned to play Jekyll and Hyde in tennis adaptations of the great story. On the flip side, Vondroušová continues to show her maturity, and Konta will rue her failures to hold when serving for each set.

39

Here it is, everything we ever dreamt of. This is where love and tennis and all you could hope for live. The wind is wildly wandering the Court Philippe Chatrier as another match between arch-rivals Rafael Nadal and Roger Federer commences. Novak Djokovic can win more Grand Slams than both men by the time they have all hung their rackets up, but the Serbian will never be as loved as these two sporting icons. This is the pairing that everyone craves, the pot of gold of tennis matchups.

They haven't played each other on clay for over half a decade. They haven't met at the French Open since 2011. Before today, Nadal won all five of their encounters. Paris may love Federer, but it hasn't been kind to this rivalry, siding only with Nadal. While Federer gets a bigger cheer, the air here swims with a soul that embraces Nadal.

Nadal in his neon, eye-damaging yellow, and Federer in his cream and cafe au lait get-up; the men are even dressed to echo their differences.

The wind is picking up, a storm a-brewing, the nature of the match not what people would hope for, as a higher power comes down to play.

Nadal is soon two games to love up; conditions mean nothing to that man. It doesn't look like it could continue to worsen, and the match keeps on going. Federer looks more hindered by the conditions than Nadal does. Nadal holds. 3-0. Both men have the poor weather; both men have obstacles. Both men's receding hair is being whipped all over their heads.

Nadal bags the first set, takes leave of the court, returns and – from nowhere – some sun splashes onto the court and then the whole atmosphere changes. The match lights up, and the crowd are hopeful the scenes before them can continue. It's an occasion, not just a Grand Slam semi-final between everyone's favourites. People want to enjoy it for that, and not have to also battle the conditions.

When Roger breaks Rafa and leads 2-0 in the second set – with the sun wearing its hat and some sublime tennis – it hits you how extraordinary that a man who is almost 38 can be playing some of his finest ever tennis. How he can hold back the ageing process, how he can never stop pushing those boundaries and the levels of discomfort of those closest to him at the top. It's simply an unbelievable return to Paris, regardless of what happens here today. Of course, maintaining form to beat Rafa over five sets on his much-loved clay, well, is this day *that* strange?

It's not just the ladies' semi-finals but also this match with its swings and roundabouts. Nadal ruins Federer's second set party and breaks back. On serve once more.

Nadal soon holds a two sets to love lead and the predictable seems to be descending again as the rain is held off. At 1-1, Federer has a howler and Nadal breaks. Federer violently launches a ball into the crowd and shows a side of himself (mostly ignored, people oblivious to what is real and what does not match with their image of perfection) that's rather uglier. Rain or shine, on clay, Nadal is on another planet to his long-time foe (and let's face it, everyone else). Federer isn't taking it well. Nadal is soon 3-1 up, three games away from the final. Yet again. He would meet either Djokovic or Thiem there.

The court is a dust bowl as Rafa waits for a wave of wind to pass to serve at 30-0 up, serving for the match. It's as though the wind is whipping up its own storm to counter and contend with Rafa's. It looks like a scene from a film... coming soon to a tennis court on a grand stage near you. He closes it out wonderfully. Next opponent, please...

It didn't provide the classic people had wanted, but it did give Roger Federer a dose of clay court reality and a much-needed, long-awaited win between the pair for Rafael Nadal, who goes on to his 12th final in the Paris Grand Slam. Twelfth. Beyond comprehension for people in and out of sport, I do not doubt.

Carried Over

On the resumption of the second men's semi-final, between Dominic Thiem and Novak Djokovic, there is an abiding feeling the match would not persist as it had the day before – under a black and grey sky and in the swirling wind – and that is quickly borne out.

Thiem struggles on serve, gets broken (having gone in last night a break up in the third set), is soon all level, and then both men go full steam ahead charging toward a third set tie-break. Even when Thiem was a break up, overnight, you knew Djokovic's reset button would allow him back into the set the same way. Thiem finds a way to break before the breaker arrives and takes the set 7 games to 5.

Rain. Again. This time Djokovic has once more levelled the match at two sets all. He turns the tables on Thiem's set three win, taking the fourth 7-5.

The rain interrupts at 4-1 to Thiem and deuce on the Djokovic serve. It's a tentative score at which to have to pause proceedings again. When they do return, Thiem wins shortly afterwards, successfully serving out over the world number one, which by now is known to be no easy task.

Rerun

The 2018 men's singles final saw Rafael Nadal play the second-best clay court player behind him, Dominic Thiem. Earlier this season, Thiem once again got a clay court win over Rafa, in the semi-final of the Barcelona Open, something he'd done now for several years running, proving his worth and that he was the closest player on clay to the Spanish supremo. The almost unbeatable giant, Nadal, could be defeated on clay and Thiem was seemingly headed for another showdown at Roland Garros with his key rival. While it did prove something, Roland Garros is not the same tournament as the others. The best-of-three set format is central to that, and both players would do well to remember that the French Open is another level up.

In some ways, it's no surprise that this year's men's Roland Garros final is a rerun of last year – the same two men squaring up to one another once more. The best two men in the world, on clay, going head to head, toe to toe, Thiem with a brand-new chance, and Nadal, going for Slam victory number 18 and many people's early prediction for the title, may well rip the heart from Thiem's chest all over again. A rerun looks likely from every which way.

Double Act

The unseeded German duo of Kevin Krawietz and Andreas Mies continued a startling ascent in doubles tennis to claim their first Grand Slam title. It was their first major outing as a partnership. The women, Kristina Mladenovic and Tímea Babos, then took their turn in the match that preceded the men's singles final. It's a special day for the Mladenovic camp, at her home major, as her boyfriend – Austria's Dominic Thiem – will take on (almost) annual champion, Rafael Nadal.

Frenchwoman Mladenovic, and Babos of Hungary, conquered on a thrilled Court Philippe Chatrier, and collected a second Grand Slam title together to add to their 2018 Australian Open doubles title, in defeating Duan Yingying and Zheng Saisai 6–2, 6–3 in the final.

A Maiden Slam Winner, Again

Ashleigh Barty (at five foot five) and Markéta Vondroušová (an inch taller) won't make up the tallest final ever played in the women's side of things, but it's another indicator of good times and wide possibilities across the women's WTA field, with winners coming from different countries, with all manner of game styles and physiques. The two women look relaxed and focussed, perhaps hiding their inner 'first time' nerves. For this is new terrain.

Australian Barty is the one who takes the chance to get her hands on some Grand Slam silverware, winning 6-1, 6-3, outplaying her opponent, holding her nerve (every inch the major winner), and having looked increasingly ready to take this gigantic leap to near the top of the women's game in recent years (and certainly months). She has swept through the draw like an Antipodean dream, with each round sharpening her arrow's aim at the title target. It has become more and more apparent, over the fortnight, that she was the heir to the Roland Garros throne. Looking back, who else could have won it? While Vondroušová, Konta, Anisimova and others did indeed impress, Barty looked the hardest to defeat, the most assured, and the one capable of taking advantage of a field that did not do what was predicted, to say the least. Vondroušová is perhaps one of those players for whom the occasion proved a little overwhelming the first time around, finally revealing her age and room for growth at the very last.

Twelfth Night

Tonight is a night for celebration. The parade is in town. With Spanish colours painting the Parisian skies, another flawless event has been seen from the best clay court player ever. Every word of praise spilled, gushed, poured over him is merited. He stood up as the best man in Paris yet again. By a country mile. By leagues. A man from another galaxy. Here, on a tennis court – unbeatable, impenetrable, gentlemanly – all hail Rafa.

Whether he gets the praise he deserves, or everyone just longs for Roger Federer, this is something *nobody* in tennis has done before. Nobody in *sport*. This achievement stands alone. One man alive knows how it feels to go beyond what would seem possible within the confines of sporting logic.

And the game has changed. This won't be repeated. Okay, I cannot guarantee that, but knowing the physicality and mental demands of the sport these days, what is needed in all departments, and at what stage you can be complete enough to contend at this highest of levels, it seems an untouchable record. The young players win less than they once did on the men's side of things. Knowing that, who could start winning titles at such a young age and then continue to do so almost every year. A fortnight. Seven matches. Best of five sets. Year after year. After year. Miracle man. A Spanish 33-year-old. Groundhog Day. The same story just becomes more and more impressive.

For who knows what lies ahead, what waiting beast would pounce. Nadal sees the trophy in his hands again and heads off into his twelfth night, a Roland Garros champion. Nothing is impossible.

The Hugely Underrated Coach That Is Conchita Martinez

The women are getting a hard time of it. With limited coaching roles for females across both the WTA and ATP tours, with battles to be paid to get the same opportunities to be on main courts at events, and new events such as The Laver Cup designed solely for the male of the tennis species, it's as clear as day. It's a man's world, a man's sport, and so on. Yet, tennis has a vast and rich history of incredible women – spectacular athletes, brilliant minds; sometimes rolled into one – who leave their marks on the game forever. This isn't to be held up beside the men or even compared with them directly. That is harmful. Women's tennis is a brilliant sport deserving of much greater praise. Many have ended careers as players, but few have gone on to coach at the highest level. Men have taken most roles as coaches to both men and women, and this has forced women out of the prominent positions. When male players such as Andy Murray, Denis Istomin, or Mikhail Kukushkin have taken on female coaches – be they a mother, wife, or someone else – it has often been regarded as a near-miraculous union. Why? A woman competing with a woman, a woman learning about tennis, has gone through the same as a man. She has built an army of tricks and an understanding of the game and its intricate soul. That knowledge can then be shared.

Martina Navratilova said, lately, that if anyone wants her wealth of top-level knowledge and experience, she would love to coach again. Quite why her expertise is not snapped up is beyond comprehension. Her career was a veritable feast of success and wonder.

In what seemed like her umpteenth Wimbledon singles final – and her last appearance there in that event – Navratilova was beaten by Conchita Martinez in the 1994 final, winning her own sole Slam.

Winning Wimbledon, any Wimbledon title, is no small accomplishment. Your name is written on the walls of the All England Club, and you are put on a global pedestal; whatever comes before and after that triumph – you are a Grand Slam champion. As such, Conchita Martinez would seem an attractive coaching proposition.

Martinez was filling in for Sam Sumyk, who was away for personal reasons, when she took her charge – Garbiñe Muguruza – to her 2017 Wimbledon title. She is now working with Karolína Plíšková and seeing an upturn in the Czech player's tempestuous form. She clearly has the right formula for positive results, is driven by exactly what makes a male coach successful – a love and knowledge of the sport – and would be able to apply her understanding of the court to any player at all.

It comes across as the most forward-thinking step on record when anyone hires a female coach these days. That is unfortunate, as it should be completely natural. Navratilova, Martinez, and an abundance of female former-professional tennis players are waiting in the wings with a wealth of experience to share. In 2019, it's astonishing that we are even discussing such a topic. If your form isn't great – man, woman, or youngster – think long and hard about making a change, and just who could help to catalyse improvements. These women have everything, and possibly even more than many male coaches do.

The Pendulum Swings

Momentum has great value in sport. It can lead an inferior sportsperson or sports team into winning positions. But when the pendulum swings back and forth between opponents, it creates a wondrous ambience of unpredictability, and excitement.

Some of the greatest encounters in sport see the pendulum swinging forth multiple times, as both players or teams find their best form at different stages or (sometimes) at the same time. The pendulum makes for breath-taking viewing, salivating scenes, and memorable action.

THE
GRASS
ELEMENT

Halle v Queens (Part 1)

At the starting gun, both the lawns of Halle and those of Queens are impeccable. Given a little spraying of sunshine, just the dose needed to feel the wrath and beauty of summer tennis, they shimmer. They are an equal feat of garden engineering.

Two weeks before the third major of the year, and the crown jewel of tennis (and certainly the grass court season), and here are two grass court adversaries wrestling for second spot behind the clearly superior major, Wimbledon.

Both Halle and Queens have long been attractive to players and to global tennis fans. Perennial Halle attendee Roger Federer is like a pied piper leading other players to a wonderful German event (not to mention one of its lesser known cities; imagine the tourism that would otherwise not occur), only to, for the most part, blow them away. He's won title after title (so far amassing nine) for years.

Queens is almost holy ground for some, among them one Andy Murray, the five-time champion. The man who, on most occasions, has held aloft surely the largest trophy in tennis. It almost dwarfs its champion each year.

Birmingham and Mallorca

Two weeks before Wimbledon, this is the time to find one's best tennis. Everyone is hunting scalps, victories to put under their belts, and confidence that enables them to feel like viable challengers for the biggest prize – the third major of the year – a trophy at the event where it all started over 150 years ago. While it clearly isn't a manageable task for all, a run of a few matches or more would light the fire for many players, too.

Before Wimbledon, Birmingham plays host to the world's current top two players – Naomi Osaka and Ashleigh Barty – and a brilliant secondary cast of other names not far behind them. This week could even see Barty take over as the new world number one, should she win the title.

Mallorca, a newer grass court tournament, meanwhile, features a compelling line up too, including Angelique Kerber, Belinda Bencic, and Sofia Kenin, making it another tournament to certainly train at least one eye upon.

Grass Grows Beneath the Feet of Legends

When contemplating the recent greats of Wimbledon – the faces who have defined many of the recent years – well, you cannot look beyond the Williams sisters, Roger Federer, Rafael Nadal, and Novak Djokovic. Not to mention Sir Andy Murray.

This year, in terms of predicting the men's winner, one of the big three would seem the logical conclusion. In the women's draw, though, there's a chance for anyone to seize the day; there has been a phenomenal range of winners thus far.

While the men's Slams often provide one of the usual suspects – and at the start of the year I predicted after a French Open Nadal win (his twelfth and final title there, in my opinion – though I hope I am wrong) that Sascha Zverev would break the pattern and win his maiden Slam, it now seems more than likely that normal service will continue.

In the ladies, it's anyone's guess. The year Petra Kvitová is having, don't be surprised if she adds to her two Wimbledon (and only Slam) titles. Or Kerber to defend. Serena to appear, and at the very least, attempt to steal the show and make it hers by finally reaching the Holy Grail of 24 titles (drawing her level with Margaret Court). Or Osaka to shine on grass, or... Karolína Plíšková, whose union with Conchita Martinez is gaining traction. If the higher-ranked Plíšková could get that serve going on grass, consistently, she'd be a hard nut to crack. And how about Muguruza, Ostapenko, Sabalenka, Bertens, Halep, Barty, Bencic, Andreescu, Konta, Vekić, and Kontaveit? Barty with her skilful and ever-improving game (and ranking) will surely have a chance on the grass at some point, if she gives herself the best glimpse at the prize. That she could now be a threat on all three surfaces is testament to how far she has come in recent times.

Pining for Chung and Rublev

Hyeon Chung and Andrey Rublev are a couple of young players who, in the past two years, have shown their worth greatly. Now, however, they find themselves frozen out of the game for one reason or another, leaving the rest of us pining their games and passion back near the top of the game, for where they seemed destined.

Remember Andrey Rublev from the US Open 2017? Just a skinny Russian 19-year-old, he looked set to take his brand of brutal hitting anywhere he wanted it to go if he learnt to stay a little calmer and focus his energy in a more contained manner. South Korean Hyeon Chung won the inaugural ATP NextGen finals in 2017 and went on to reach the semi-finals of the next Slam, the 2018 Australian Open. He and Rublev looked set to battle things out with the other talented young guns for the coming decade and change.

However, reality bites and delivers tough lessons and circumstances that leave many reeling. The body will bow, and the body will break. Rublev had a lower back stress fracture, and Chung his own back issues. Injuries can be an arduous journey to come back from at any age, and both men have had their portion of time side-lined. All we can hope, is to see them fit and healthy and on the world's biggest stages again very soon, as they deserve to be.

Andy Murray Returns to The Court

Queens Club this year has many appealing factors, none less than Andy Murray making a clear comeback statement in the doubles event on the evening of Thursday 20th June (delayed by a day due to inclement weather). It's the English summer, the grass court tournaments and the meaning of seeing Andy Murray taking to the professional tennis court – approximately four months after having hip-replacement surgery – is something not lost on anyone. There is little time in England to make the most of the tennis season, although much of the grass court season still resides within its walls. This return, of a knight no less, only adds to the attention Queens receives this week and the anticipation tennis fans have. They want to see Murray back on court. That he and his partner, Spaniard, Feliciano López, go on to defeat the top doubles seeding for the week of Juan Sebastián Cabal and Robert Farah is symbolic of the seriousness of this attempt, and the man that Murray is in general.

It's wonderful to eye Murray on a tennis court, on a green lawn, with all the splendid Queens Club and Wimbledon memories we have of him. He is (somewhat typically) clad in dark colours, standing out, compared to the other three on-court players in white.

It doesn't feel like Murray is saying 'farewell', more that he is easing his way back in, both as advised and as his body tells him to approach things with caution. This isn't a swansong as he heads off into the sunset; the man loves to compete, and for however long it might remain a possibility, he will persevere. He wants to battle it out. Nobody could deny he wants one-to-one combat as well as doubles, and Queens is a reasonable way of measuring where he is at, and what he is capable of. Let's face it, who wouldn't love to see him get his hands on that giant Queens trophy in the singles one more time?

The Federer Effect (Parts 2 and 3)

Jo-Wilfried Tsonga grows into his second-round encounter with Roger Federer to almost – but not quite – put the seasoned Swiss, and nine-time champion, out in his second home of Halle.

While Federer does go on to win, it is an abnormally poor day at the office for Mr. Federer, and he more than offered Tsonga a chance to seize the victory. The Frenchman simply didn't take it. He will be kicking himself, without doubt. Roger, missing shots he rarely does, looked a shadow of his usual self, and will certainly want to improve his game for the next round. Tsonga, closing in on a magical win, perhaps smelled the shock and tightened up, remembered who it was across the net, froze, and then found himself unable to replicate what had got him into such a tantalising position. The Federer Effect in all its stark glory.

Against lesser players, Tsonga would likely have closed out this win. Before a ball is hit, as with Serena and Novak, for example, Federer already has an advantage. The psychological factor that has opponents running scared, their minds rattled and riddled with thoughts of the impossible rival.

Against Tsonga, Federer could be found, once again, mastering the art of hanging tough when things weren't going well; turning the 'against' to the 'for', ultimately murdering the flow his opponent had discovered. A flood diverted; a disaster for Federer and his legion of fans averted.

The following day, things are different and yet not. The match against Roberto Bautista Agut doesn't feel the same as the match of the previous round, though both Federer's opponents in the two matches fight back from a set down and work their ways into winning positions, but The Federer Effect has much the same result. The Swiss comes out on top and reaches the semi-finals of an event he loves – well, who wouldn't with this level of success – yet again.

This time, Bautista Agut is on the receiving end of a defeat that might potentially cause nightmares. The Spaniard giving a brilliant and fearless display on grass, showing no nerves whatsoever, responding well to going a set down, and fighting back, giving himself a chance, just like Tsonga. He has his chances, but ultimately sees it all swim by; an almost imagined window of possibility. Federer is winning ugly, despite his beautiful game.

The Palace of Future Regrets

Nick Kyrgios is building a palace. A place to hold archives of endless regrets, stained with bad behaviour and disrespect overshadowing his immense (and clearly intense) tennis gift. Felix Auger-Aliassime, 18, today shows himself to be more mature and mentally able to meet the task than the 24-year old Kyrgios, as both young men must play twice in one day. Yes, we all develop at different rates, but you cannot help but feel Kyrgios' job of self-sabotage is perfectly executed. There is no change in approach to what he has been doing for years, and those desperate to see his tennis garner the attention and take the plaudits – instead of what he is proffering – are left wanting.

The Australian Kyrgios is indubitably one of the most talented players of his generation, if not of any. At times, it catches the viewer how breathtakingly skilled he is, his natural talent symbolising perhaps an all-time tennis gift. Wrapping that up with mental strength, a hard work ethic and passion, too, is what makes a player the whole package. Kyrgios' vision and hand-eye skill are astonishing. It's a shame his attitude and approach to tennis doesn't quite pair up with those attributes.

While taking shots at proven masters as well as legends of the game, in recent times, and being caught up in headlines for almost all the wrong reasons, there is no sign of an end to the antics. The constant stream of shenanigans and mischief show him stuck on a road to nowhere. Everyone is wishing for the penny to drop, while he stubbornly builds a palace of anything except the wins he is capable of. It's tough to watch him these days, such is the likelihood of something ugly rearing its head. Let us hope it is not always so.

Another Combustion for Zverev the Younger

David Goffin, on his day, loves collecting the scalp of a top-five player. The ATP Finals a couple of years ago saw him take out Nadal and Federer (albeit at the end of a long season for both men) on his way to losing in the final, in London, to Grigor Dimitrov.

Enter Alexander Zverev, with his bags loaded with glimmering promise, pulling against his abilities; an inner tug-of-war that will hopefully be resolved before his best time has passed.

While Goffin seems to relish such matches, Zverev gives the impression of a man carrying around weighty expectations everywhere he goes. Shaking that ghost free might be the key to winning majors. With Tsitsipas smelling blood and heading in tunnel-vision fashion for the apex of the game, not to mention the even younger Felix Auger-Aliassime, and others who are encroaching on his terrain with almost unfathomable speed now, Zverev has talked about being under pressure as the young hope everyone pinned their hopes on. Expectation seems to hang around his neck, a shining anchor – like one of his gold chains – pulling him down to the bottom of the sea.

Zverev wins the first set against Goffin reasonably well (6-3) and surrenders the second easily (1-6). The men then keep it together to find their ways to the latter part of the set. A final set tie-break looms; one of these players will momentarily exit a winner and one a loser. The decider commences.

At 1-1, it's no clearer who will take which role. Goffin begins to overcome Zverev, though, and homes in on victory in front of his rival's support. At 3-6, with Zverev serving, Goffin has three match points over the higher-seeded German. It's soon done and dusted; Goffin cementing a return to form with a big win.

Halle and Queens (Part 2)

While Karen Khachanov and one of Germany's own, Jan-Lennard Struff, enter into a final set now under the centre court roof at Halle, Stanislas Wawrinka and home player Dan Evans have had to stop for more English rain at the Queens Club in London with the Swiss 5-3 up and serving for the first set.

Halle has a roof and can keep things going. Queens, as yesterday, must wait, hoping for the dark skies to clear up.

And Struff, rather unexpectedly after winning the first set tie-break, has got Khachanov's number. He's in the form of his life, seeking a Wimbledon seeding; he is pushing on, solving the on-court problems he faces and blossoming. In his late twenties. It's like a snake shaking past skins; shedding those memories, and finding new and better versions each time.

As the match progresses, inseparable as they are, the third set looks like wearing shades of a Grecian tragedy that one man must lose. It's tight, as the flowing tennis between the two men crescendos and reaches its culmination. Khachanov doesn't prevail, as one might have expected. But his standing in the top ten is entirely justified, and he is often able to come through matches like this when a year or two ago he wasn't as consistent. Today, however, it is not to be, and the home player advances, in great form just prior to Wimbledon.

Queens is in Wimbledon's back yard, providing players with the luxury of being down the road and already based in London prior to the year's major grass court tournament. The English weather and mood in summer is a unique thing; summer not always appearing, and loaded with pre-Brexit apocalyptic charm.

Halle is little more than a stone's throw away. Growing into a stunning venue that looks more like a grass court Masters – and, boy, are we missing one of those. It would be the obvious choice of venue if there was to be one.

Stefanos Tsitsipas is the number one seed at an ATP 500 event (here in Queens). That is big news, signalling what he has become and what he will be for long into the future of tennis. Felix Auger-Aliassime is now on the cusp of the top 20, after entering the top 100 only earlier this year. In his breakthrough year, he looks set to be heading straight for the top ten even by the year-end. If he continues this form (perhaps a task too tall), he might even be in London come November. This rise is astronomical and even more unexpected than Tsitsipas' own incredible rise a year earlier. The Canadian is two years the Greek's junior. And while he has some messy and weird shots, he builds further blocks, putting together a sterling body of work in 2019, with every week, every single match. The kid is an ace machine, firing down bullets for fun. Little darts of love destined to sound on the backboards. They skid off the grass and up into the air beyond any possible racket contact, much to opposing players' dismay.

A barnstormer of a tight semi-final between Matteo Berrettini and David Goffin took place on the penultimate day in Halle. Nobody could say the two men didn't deserve their berths in the final four. Khachanov and Zverev, respectively, might have looked – on paper – more likely to meet at this stage, but their conquerors more than made the stage their own. They showed why they, and not their higher-ranked counterparts of the day before, were playing in front of a packed crowd in Halle.

Several breakpoints on the serve of each player in the second set are not taken until Berrettini serves at 3-4. No break of serve yet for the match that had seen Goffin capture the first set on a tie-break and now, failing at 15-40, Goffin breaks with his second break point of the game. Goffin will serve for the match.

Apart from some quality tennis, Goffin's experience and level-headedness are what see him win in two. He will likely take on Roger Federer – who faces Pierre-Hughues Herbert – for a chance at the title tomorrow.

Switching to Queens, the first semi-final there reveals Daniil Medvedev and Gilles Simon to be in an equally close first set. Simon on serve goes from 0-30 to winning the game with the next four points; a tie-break will decide the opener. The quality is high and whoever loses it, as Berrettini did in Halle, may well not recover. Queens and Halle are pretty close to one another, and deciding on which tournament is best is a push. What is true, is that they are two brilliant tournaments, and either way, they are the two best grass court warm-ups for Wimbledon on the men's side of things.

Unlike the straight sets wins for Federer and Goffin in their respective Halle semi-finals, Medvedev is taken to a final set, with a sense of irritation settling within him. Simon continues to frustrate and wind up Medvedev, as if he were a child's toy, that he then watches lose it. The Russian goes off in a fit and burst of wild energy. Simon stays on course and claims the victory 6-7, 6-4, 6-3.

Baselines

After a week of action, the baselines are worn to a grey-brown hue, the tough soil revealed, the earth-like patches where grass turns yellow and resembles a meeting of two worlds, foreign lands. The yellow fades into green, on the lesser explored areas of the court, where tennis shoes tread less often. Further in, there is still green – sombre in colour; the heatwave mars its natural spirit.

Halle Open Men's Final

Goffin's shots look almost as punchy those of Federer. Both men start by serving well, giving little away. Soon it is two games all, as the court is bathed in golden sunshine, and a perfect blue sky hangs overhead. The centrepiece of the Halle event is well underway.

The week has had the impression of being Federer's again – coming close to exiting all week and prevailing each round instead – and when the wily Swiss takes another tie-break with ease and then breaks at the start of set two, a tenth title looks assured. We all know the outcome. We have been here before on many occasions. He will be the man with the most title wins so far this year and he is reaching the latter stages of every tournament he enters, unable to be toppled from his pedestal near the top of the game. That he is soon to celebrate his 38th birthday means nothing. There is no age. Only passion, life, love for these moments, from all angles.

The fact that age deteriorates us mere mortals doesn't apply to Federer, it seems, as he marches into Wimbledon and goes hunting for a ninth title there. It's going to be hard to stop him. If anything has been learned this week (and this season), it's that if you get a glimmer of hope, against the Swiss maestro, take it, or live to regret the day you didn't.

Birmingham Classic Ladies' Final

At the Birmingham Classic Ladies' final, the lawn is still a fresh green – there has been more rain of late, and less sun to bombard those darkened blades. The lawn also shows few ventures to the net this week and resembles something utterly different to the grass of Halle, for example, on this day of finals.

And it's a rare thing to witness a match in which one player could become the new world number one (for the first time), if they win. Current world number two, Ashleigh Barty, taking on her friend, Julia Görges, also wears something of destiny (much as Federer's win did a little earlier). Barty does claim the prize (winning 6-3, 7-5), and she assumes the ultimate mantle in tennis. Ashleigh Barty will go into Wimbledon very much the player to beat.

The Lopez-Simon Final Showpiece (Queens Final)

The final between Gilles Simon and Feliciano López at Queens has everything the routine Federer win in Halle is missing. Simon, close to losing, takes it to a second set tie-break and levels the match – reeling off five points in a row from 2-4 down at the change of ends. Queens' chief court looks less worn than the one in Halle. It's seen rain this week and has had singles and doubles as often as it could. Rain didn't interrupt more than a day and a half at the start of the week.

Equally, there is an air of inevitability here – that it is Lopez's day again – and in the final set tie-break, the Spaniard doesn't mess up the way he did in the second set breaker. It's a pearl of a final and, Lopez, who gets his name etched into Queens folklore once more, at 37, will later play the doubles final. In his second final of the day, he will go on to win alongside his partner for the week, Andy Murray (on his own return to the professional tennis courts).

Headlines from the Week

Unluckiest man in Tennis, Del Potro, scores yet another injury

Twins hard to separate (Kristýna Plíšková prevails in first ever professional battle between twins)

Schwartzman Clubs Čilić On Grass

Barty Keeps on Winning

Kerber Tunes Up ready for Wimbledon Title Defence

Federer Nearly Loses but Never Quite Does

Teenager Auger-Aliassime Continues to Surge Towards the Top

Feliciano Lopez Plays Three Times in One Day, Wins the Lot

The Art of Tennis II Summary

The Swan Show 2018/19 has ended. While the loop is familiar, the scenes within have further captured the imaginations of tennis fans across the planet; a deep well of surprises and magic, drama and supreme athleticism.

Naomi Osaka was the first woman to win back-to-back majors in over two years in the ladies' game. Novak Djokovic's attempt to win four straight majors was thwarted only by Dominic Thiem on clay who then ran into the brick wall of Rafael Nadal in the final, with the Spaniard claiming his twelfth title on the Parisian dirt. Roger Federer didn't win a Grand Slam but did wow many crowds and spectators with his clinical brand of seductive and mind-boggling tennis, a thing of beautiful craft. In short, the Big Three were irrepressible.

Serena Williams didn't claim major title number 24, but she did come close, putting herself in the reckoning, looking like a future danger in any event she would enter. There were several high-profile breakthroughs for Ashleigh Barty, Daniil Medvedev, Bianca Andreescu, Felix Auger-Aliassime, and Markéta Vondroušová. As the decade draws to a close, a changing of the guard in both the women's and men's games has become increasingly evident, causing both excitement for the new, and sadness for the passing of a stupendous era now in its final stages.

There was the polemical, the predictable, and the popular across the familiar venues of the tennis tour. The year was seasoned with unexpected spices, adding a fresh and unforeseen flavour, ending just prior to the commencement of Wimbledon 2019, where the next instalment – The Art of Tennis III – will pick up the baton.

The Swan Show Reprise

An entrance. Graceful, as if in a dream. Nothing else exists, only the journey, only this path, this exquisite acting out of fate, those playing their parts to precision, par excellence. And swans are gliding, and swans are bursting into life, unexpectedly, claiming fruits, until an exit and tranquillity. The dream collapsed, faded, vanished. Until next time. Until we meet again.

The courts of Wimbledon and the SW19 club site, in general, nurture the idea of nature within the sport. The three preceding grass court weeks bring to the tennis public's attention the switch from hard and clay courts, and there is a sharpness to the players in white upon the green lawns that is incomparable to what is experienced elsewhere.

The old stands holding up the young closable roof, the dark forest green of the arena, and the vibrant grass of the lawns – the surroundings as close to natural-coloured ones as any tennis event sees; there is something indefinitely poetic about this corner of the tennis world.

Snapping at their heels, was the vivid imagery of a dream. As if it were chasing them...

When, finally, the brand-new Wimbledon advert comes on the television, it is a memorable and veritable feast, it ignites excitement across the spectrum of ages – of tennis fans and more. For the third Grand Slam of the year opens new doors to fans of sport, of art, of beauty. It touches on the old and the new – of tradition, of music, of concept, and, of course, inspires memories of past tennis players and scenes, swans to long be remembered. Nothing else exists, only the journey, only this path, this exquisite acting out of fate, those playing their parts to precision.

Other Books from Bennion Kearny

Togetherness: How to Build a Winning Team

This concise and practical book – from Dr Matt Slater, a world authority on togetherness – shows people how to develop togetherness in their teams. The journey starts with an understanding of what underpins togetherness and how it can drive high performance and well-being simultaneously. It then moves onto practical tips and activities based on the 3R model (Reflect, Represent, Realise) that readers can learn and complete with their teams to unlock their togetherness.

One Football, No Nets

In September 2017, amateur British football coach Justin Walley became the "National Team" Manager of Matabeleland, an obscure international team in western Zimbabwe. Before him lay the seemingly impossible task of taking his group of unknown amateur footballers from an impoverished region of Africa to the "alternative world cup" – the CONIFA World Football Cup in London, the following summer. All that stood in his way was the small matter of no money, no resources, no salary, no visas, and no sponsors. There was one football, though… but no goal nets.

Lightning Source UK Ltd.
Milton Keynes UK
UKHW020624091219
355034UK00013B/1401/P